Trapped An Invasion by a Human Predator

Trapped An Invasion by a Human Predator

Maggie Brown-Rogers

authorHOUSE®

AuthorHouse™
1663 Liberty Drive
Bloomington, IN 47403
www.authorhouse.com
Phone: 1 (800) 839-8640

Published by AuthorHouse   04/29/2015

ISBN: 978-1-5049-0961-7 (sc)
ISBN: 978-1-5049-0959-4 (e)

Library of Congress Control Number: 2015906598

Print information available on the last page.

Any people depicted in stock imagery provided by Thinkstock are models, and such images are being used for illustrative purposes only. Certain stock imagery © Thinkstock.

This book is printed on acid-free paper.

In memory of the Late:
Evelyn Lene Brown
03/25/1941-03/15/1990

This book is dedicated to all of the prayer warriors that solicited a prayer toward Heaven for the Flower Girl.

Acknowledgments

First of all, I would like to thank God for allowing me the opportunity to use my life experience, to help someone that is stuck in the transition of moving forward. Then, I would like to take the time to thank my parents although mother is resting. I would like to thank each and every one of my siblings. In addition, I would like to extend a special thanks to the members of New Jerusalem Seventh-day Adventist church for all the prayers that was petitioned in my name.

Next, I would like to take the time to thank the people over the years that extended an ear when; I needed it the most. Certainly, you have given me more courage than; you could ever imagine. After all, it was you who allowed me to narrate this story-line. Also, I would like to thank the people that waited patiently on me to open up. You see. Many times, we can open packages, which should be left closed; but thank God this package was worth revealing.

Last but not least, I would like to thank every victim that has used their tragedy to motivate someone else in a positive way. As we all know, life has its ups and downs; however, our mission on earth is to reach out to others that need us most. Sometimes, our mission may carry us through rough patches before; we reach the smooth soil. Nonetheless these rough moments in life are there to build us up; so that when the bridge of life buckles, we can with-stand the storm. Truly, I **THANK GOD!** I was not consumed during the brewing of my storm. Let's continue to pray that God keep you through yours.

CHAPTER 1

The Sacrifice

I grew up in a small city outside the walls of East. St. Louis, Illinois. I was blessed to have the warmth of a two parent home, and a great deal of siblings. Even in the early years of my life, I realized. I was different from my sisters and brothers. True enough, I loved my family with my whole heart. But, I began to drift into a small world of my own. At an early age, I began. What some would say was a peculiar relationship with a stranger? Bizarre as it may seem, I felt comfortable with the closeness; we shared. I was not ashamed to tell others: he was a true friend of mine. In fact, I spent many hours of the day building a relationship with him, which someday would be my only hope of survivor. Likewise, he was just attentive to me.

Although I loved the outdoors and looked forward to outdoor activities, the indoor was my idea of happiness. I knew the noise level from outside would break my concentration inside. It was not that I was all that different from other children. Without a doubt, I enjoyed the hobbies of jumping rope, playing basketball, and just everyday play. Yet, reading was my favorite hobby. Therefore, I looked forward to the inside chores. I would read stories after stories, memorizing as much material as my brain could absorb. This was one of the best moments of my life. Nevertheless, it was nothing like the time; I would spend with my savior. Oh! How I treasured the richness of his presence?

Day after day, I longed to be in the arms of the savior. Strange as it may seem, I know; he enjoyed my company too. It was like spending time with my best friend. Nonetheless, this friend was like no other. I could talk to him about anything my heart desired. There was never a time when; he ignored my plea. So, I spent the majority of my free time, gaining the knowledge to be a helpful individual to those that needed me.

As I began to mature in age and grow spiritually, the communication expanded even more. Many people would say; I was wise beyond my years. It was at that time; I realized. God was strengthening me, for the battle of my life. No doubt, I thought the battle was to run for Jesus. So I started the mission of building up a strong relationship with God, as the devil plotted pointlessly to bring me down to my knees. Rest assured, I never feared the Devil, or the plans he thought; he could use to sabotage my life. So I continued to reach to higher heights and deeper depth. It was not about the religion; some thought I had. I knew in my heart; it was about the relationship, which someday would test my faith.

Struggling to understand God's purpose, I prayed daily for answers to be revealed about his son, and how humble he was to his father. Many times, I wondered. Why God had chosen me? However, I knew the day would come, and my faith would be tried by the fire. Oh! How I wanted to prove. I was really ready. It was no doubt that I could conquer whatever came my way. So I constantly reminded God. I was ready for the battle. Moreover, I was armed for the war. Trusting that God would deliver, I asked him to place me in whatever setting. He saw fit. Quite often, I asked him to let his will be done. Yet many times, he reminded me; he was still working out things on my behalf. I believed. He was God, and I wanted more than anything to prove. I could be humble and obedient. But the more I surrendered, the more he reemphasized that my day was still to come.

In my heart, I knew. I was a missionary fighting for a good cause. So I longed even more to be just like Jesus.

Although I was young, I had very little in common with my peers. It was no doubt that I was different from the way; they were. Not that I was abnormal. I just had a different outlook about the things, which was important to me. It was not about popularity, but getting acquainted with this stranger. My parents had befriended.

At that time, summers were very long, and hot. The sun appeared to literally burn the top layer of your skin. Sweat would pour from the body, giving the illusion. Our bodies were dissolving from the intense heat. Oh! But I enjoyed those hot summers. It was a time of recuperating from the bitter cold winters. Indeed, it was a time to warm up physically and spiritually, and let the fire flow through my soul. These were the days when; children were children. For the most part, they were mindful of their actions and had respect for one another. Likewise, parents were parents in those days. They were active in all aspects of their children's lives. In addition, neighbors were the eyes for the young. Church folks were involved in helping one another. In those days, school teachers worked beyond just teaching. They were self-motivated about the welfare of the children in their surrounding communities. Moreover, those were the days; families showed a true sign of togetherness.

Growing up in a very poor community, I took pleasure in the time. I spent at church. This was an event that allowed us, as a family to spend the day away from home. So every Saturday, our parents would prepare us to worship with fellow believers. This was a time, which. I could learn more about God, and the desires. He had for my life. For most of the young children in our congregation, Sabbath school was the most interesting part of the day. However,

I enjoyed the moment of worship. This was my cue to find out even more about. The God I often prayed to.

As the preacher would bless the congregation with the word, I carefully took notes as he painted. His vision of; who God was? I was so moved by the sermons that I would play them back and forth, in my mind like a human tape recorder. It was an invitation for God himself to dwell in me. I wanted to be filled with as much of the Holy Spirit as God would allow. At this time, the only dream I had was to live for Jesus. Slowly the sun began to set; our day of worship was coming to a close. I can remember being so excited. I couldn't wait to share all the great news. I had learned with my friends. Often times, Saturday nights would slip away peaceful, because the majority of the day was spent in the house of worship. It was like a reunion, and I looked forward to it every week.

Bright and early on Sunday mornings, I would rise up, give thanks to God for all his blessings, and indeed. They were blessings. I knew that I had a long week ahead. But I had to hold on to the message to carry me through. I had to challenge myself to be strong, and trust God to deliver. Moreover, I knew the Devil would defy me also. Unsure of what each day would bring, I continued to embrace the God that I served. Eagerly waiting for the middle of the week, I knew; once again, we would be reunited as one. Prayer service for the foundation of the church, which I attended, was every Wednesday. But with limited gas and inadequate funds, our parents elected to have service at home in our living room. There was no such thing as missing in action. In addition, tardiness did not exist. There were no excuses outside of being sick. In other words, Wednesday night prayer service was a requirement, not a recommendation.

Giving a double dose of unity weekly, I was able to keep God close to my heart. I truly loved him, and his son Jesus. And I wanted more than anything to show him how much. I visualize; what he was like? Although his outer appearance was never part of my apparition, I wanted to have the characteristics of God, my father, and I prayed for him to show me favor. Unlike many children in my age group, I had no desire to be strapped down by the cares of the world. I wanted more than anything to be a witness to the best prosecutor, the world would ever know. So I pleaded my case before God, and he endorsed my decision. At last, it was evident that I was part of the team. Even though I was a little reserved, shyness was never part of my vocabulary. I was proud to be a soldier. Furthermore, I was enthused to stand up and be counted.

CHAPTER 2

Dreams And Premonitions

Then around the age of nine, life began to change for me. I was never a slothful, lazy individual, but I stayed tired all the time. It was at those times. God would reveal himself through dreams for my purpose. These times were important to me, because they allowed God to talk to me in private. These were the best moments of my life. I had been promoted; I was no longer a private in his army. My rank had been advance; my goodwill had been granted. At first, the dreams were mere images of small things, before they took place. Simple things such as family surprise visits. Even though, some people viewed this as intuition. It was not that simply. The dreams were coming too often. The visions were coming to pass. Then, things became more complex; it was no longer uncomplicated things; death had shown; it true colors.

Confused about what was taking place, I watched for signs hoping each event would be proven wrong. But time and time again, the dreams became a reality. The end result was assured. The revelation was revealed. It was then that it was indisputable. God was showing me true signs and wonders. He was using me to prepare the news of some of the things that would come to pass. I was content that God saw fit to trust me. But I was perplexed. As to how, I would convince others. I was a dreamer.

No doubt, I wanted to tread carefully across the pathway. I realized that it was easy for others to question my sanity. So I was cautious about exposing these dreams. Because often times, people are known to open packages, which should have been kept closed. Therefore, I concealed the things that were entrusted in me, for quite a while. Nevertheless, the dreams didn't go away. In fact, they began to increase in revelation. I am not saying…I had a dream every day. Nonetheless, I know; they came as frequently as a good summer breeze. Likewise, sometimes, they would exit as quickly as they arrived. Though some may see dreams as strange or unusual, I knew God often used dreams or parables to get his point across. Consequently, I believed that this was his way of accomplishing his mission.

Motivated to aid God in every means possible, I was open -minded to let him have his way in my life. Yet, the dreams persisted. Powerful as the mind is, I knew. God was even more influential. So I never question his judgment. I never made an inquiry about his plans. I was only a small vessel used for the preparation of enlighten. Although some people proclaim to be psychics, palm readers, and practice witch craft, I knew these things were against the principles of God's teaching. Therefore, I never took credit for them. Nonetheless, there was no question. I was convinced. The dreams were real. These were not coincidence; neither were they dreams from a lack of sleep. Persuaded by something within, I had to at some point share this good news with others. But what would be my approach? Who could I trust? What would they think about me? For a moment, I battle with this decision. Aware that mentally illness was unacceptable, how could I disprove the judgment? What if my sanity came into play? Who would come to my rescue? These were the questions, which pondered me.

In my heart, I felt like. I had to find the only true person; I could confide in. Slowly as I approached the bedroom of my parents, the question wavered in the back of my mind. What would she think of this quiet, reserved daughter? Would questions arise about? What was going through my head? Or would she instantly run me for medical treatment, as she often did with all of her children?

What would the end results be for our relationship? All these questions came into play, so I relented and return to my room.

Still the dreams were there, I had to get a grip on. What would be my next move? It was evident that I had to share, the episodes of these dreams at some point. But until then, I waited for further instructions. I waited on the next vision. I wanted to be mindful and not step outside of the will of God. Equally, I was careful not to step outside of the walls of protection. Meanwhile, I kept a prayer close to my heart. Even more, the dreams came. Once again, I gathered the nerves to trust my mother. I always knew. She had a strong belief that God was real, and his standards were genuine. Careful, I peeked around the corner of her bedroom. Our parent's bedroom was a unit, which separated the girls and boys rooms. Therefore, I didn't have any other rooms to crossover. It was at this time; I glared into the eyes of the most precious soul. God could have ever placed in my life. It was my mother, my best friend. I could see life through her eyes. The confirmation had been allowed. I knew. I could reveal my true self to her. The secret was no longer hush-hush. It was a relief to share. What I had been keeping from the rest of the world all this time?

Indeed, I could breathe a sigh of relief. The dreams were no longer only my secret. Mom was amazed about. What God had done, and the things he had disclosed? I was astonished that she never questioned my integrity. She never doubted the visions. It was like… she had been warned of this moment. There was no surprise. Oh! I could truly tell you. Her heart appeared to have some knowledge of; what my secret was before hand?

From that day on, I continued to share my dreams with her. I would sit at the foot of her bed, and we would talk as much as. I needed it. She was never too busy, always attentive like a good mother should. God had given me a great mother and even a better friend. Many times, I would unveil my dreams to her, and we would search for interpretation. In the event, she was unsure. She would telephone her mother, which considered herself a dream interpreter.

No doubt, I listened; I have to be honest. I was not always sure her interpretation was correct. But, sometimes things did happen according to her revelation. Consequently I remained open-minded. Moreover, I considered her conclusion. But then the dreams were no longer dreams about others. I had received a premonition that hit home. This dream had moved into my comfort zone. I had always been taught from a young child not to question God. Therefore, I respected the wisdom, which had been shared with me, and entrusted his will be done. I was strong for a young child. Nevertheless, the dream was bothersome.

How would I respond to a revelation that would change the rest of my life? I had to consider. What was in the best interest for me? What would the family's future hold if the result from the dream was not in my favor? Unlike some people, I knew; this was selfish. I couldn't think of a time. I even deliberated about interfering with God's plan. So how could I not trust him now? At that point, I was able to move from the thought of even attempting to plead my case before God. Reality had set in. I knew that I was about to be a sacrifice. But what kind of sacrifice, I was still unaware? Based on the promises of Jesus, I had no reason to fear. I had to go on, because I trusted him. I had seen God in action too many times. So I had a guarantee that **"If God was for me it shouldn't matter who was against me"**. There was no need to consider the foe.

I thought about Jesus and the broken heart of his father. Then, the picture was clear. What made me more important than anyone else? Just at the time, I realized. I was going to be tempted, and there was no turning back. Holiness was upon me, and I was building myself up spiritually. I knew at some point. Satan would have his way with me, but the victory wouldn't be in his favor. I utilized this time to view a few of the Bible stories. I always wanted to be like Jesus, and have the faith of Job. So the next twelve to nineteen hours, I prayed for help from on high. I knew my strength. Yet, I knew the skillful treats of old Satan. Wise as many thought, I was for my years. I couldn't explain the dream. This one was different. It was beyond. What my wisdom would permit?

The mathematician in me could not divide the number. No science lab could teach me how to breakdown this molecule. It wasn't a teacher on earth that could have taught me how to pass this exam. So I leaned closer to the instructor; who I knew could make me understand? The day was Wednesday morning. This was the day; I usually received my double dose of spiritual guidance, for the duration of the week. As I started my daily routine of praying and supplication, once again, my mind drifted off to the dream from last night. I pondered with the decision to reveal the dream to my mother, and decided against the matter. Then, I started out to school, which was my normal routine. This school day was just like any other day. There were no visible signs of trouble. In other words, I enjoyed the peaceful day with my peers. But the end of the school day was approaching; soon, it would be time to return home.

After arriving home, I always prepare myself for homework assignment, and household chores. By this time, my other siblings would have arrived, and dinner would be served. This was a normal custom in our household, and Wednesdays were no exceptions. Hours were passing rapidly, it was time for pray service to begin. I arrived in the living room about 6:55 p.m. As I waited for the rest of my siblings to arrive, I felt myself caught up in a world of my own. It was a tradition for us to open up prayer meeting with a word of prayer. Then, we would go straight into our song service. After which, we would closed with a word of prayer. Oh! This was the best prayer meeting over the many years. I had every attended. I cried as I song from the depth of my heart; **"Pass me not Oh! Gentle Savior hear my humble cry while on others there are calling do not pass me by"**.

Indeed, I was delighted to be a part of God's team. I never would have ever imagined the peace, which he had showered on me that evening. Finally, the service had ended. The one hour prayer meeting was quickly gone, as rapidly as it came. I gathered my Bible as I marched headed to my mother's room. Once again, I was led by the Holy Spirit to prepare her for the unknown. How would she react? The dream was not just a dream any longer. It would interrupt her livelihood. The dream would rearrange her life. It was no longer a dream about other people. God had chosen me, and there would be no turning back. Would she still hold on to the faith in the God? She loved. Or would she reject his will? Would she be like Moses? Or would her heart be like that of a Judas?

So as I approached her, I comfortably sat at the foot of her bed. She looked into my eyes. I always wondered; could she have seen signs of something that would come to pass? Or was she just giving her undivided attention to me? Who would ever know? It was a strange setting. However, I told her about my dream. She never uttered a word. She only stared at me. I couldn't say much of anything, because I hadn't been giving any more instructions. In fact, I was clueless; as to what, my fate would hold. To be honest with you, I never gave it a second thought. I could only wait on him to reveal himself. I could only be patient until. He decided the day had arrived. It was evident that my time, was not his time, and the preparation had not been completed.

CHAPTER 3

The Kidnapping

The next day was as peaceful as the prayer service. There was nothing usual about this day at all. I went on about my normal duties praying, attending school, studying, worshiping, and chatting on the telephone. It was like… my mind had been redirected away for relaxation. It was just wholesome tranquility. I have to admit. I enjoyed every moment. Night fall came quickly, I rested well; in fact, the hours of sleep was not disturb at all. There were no dreams. Likewise, there were no visions, just pure pleasure. I was delighted.

At sunrise Friday morning, I prepare myself for prayer and devotion. I looked forward to Fridays. I was granted the opportunity to join my two older sisters. They were high school students. As we all know, high school could be very costly. Furthermore, it was no secret. We were dirt poor. In addition, mom was a very sick lady, but she was creative. It was these creations that help cut the cost of living. She would make flowers for the two of them to sell, which help decrease the cost of their high school years. So on Fridays, they would pick me up from the elementary school. We would head to the business area to exchange the goods for a profit.

Family was important to me, and I enjoyed this time with my sisters. I was proud to feel needed, and even more than thankful. I could help out. But I have to be honest. I adored the outing even more. I could skip the regular home cooked meal, and take pleasure in my favorite "The Famous City Burger". Although our parents were not there physically, I knew that obedience would provide for me a next time. So, I respected the rules of my sisters. Also, I was blessed with a speech, before I was allowed to accompany them each week. I was never a troubled child, and tried as much as possible to keep my word. Therefore,

I would ask for permission to walk to the hamburger stand a couple blocks away for my famous meal. As always, my wish was granted.

However, this day was different. I was approached by a guy that had an interest in the flowers, which I was carrying. He stated, "He would love to buy some for his wife". He requested that I come to his apartment approximately a few feet away. He appeared to be kind, humble, and innocent. Furthermore, I was never told that there were bad people in society. It is unclear to me whether my parents thought all people had some good qualities. Or they lived an illusion that faith would shield our family from dangerous situations. In other words, I didn't have any reasons to be raising a red flag. Likewise, I wasn't aware; my life was hanging in a balance. So, I followed him into the apartment.

Yes, I was naïve; but I take no responsibility for his actions. I was only a twelve year-old child. Wisdom was no longer in my favor. In addition, I was outside the walls of safety. I had no idea of; what he wanted with me? But I was sure of one thing. The dream had become a nightmare. It turned out… I was going to be a pawn for the devil. My heart was crushed; my life was over, and my will had been broken. I declare; it is not easy to be collateral for the devil. The next few hours would be the longest hours of my life. Oh! How I cried; I screamed. I pleaded for him to allow me to walk away. But the appeal was returned void. He had a lot of hurt built up in him, and I could see the emptiness in his eyes. I stood there with tears in my eyes, as he ordered me to remove my clothes. Strange as it may seem, and impossible as it to believe, I still was unaware of his plans. For the most part, I knew. They were new to me, and I was uncomfortable with the setting. As a result,

I had become a broken trophy, for this sick, hateful, angry, and murderous low-life of a man.

So I tried to entice him by telling him about my older sisters a couple blocks away. But of course, he rejected the information. Do not think for one moment… I would have ever exposed my sisters to this despicable animal. I was looking for a way out. After which, I offered him the two dollars that I had in my pocket. Also, he rejected the money. Once again, the level of wisdom that I had acquired, at the time didn't work.

I was no challenge for this beast, and as a result, the torture began. I couldn't perform the things; he requested of me. Therefore, this made him furious. Yet, he failed to realize. I had no experience in this area. In fact, I had only seen one male unclothed, and I can honestly say; it was foreign to me. Several weeks before, a guy had motion me to his car. I thought; it was to make a transaction; but when I arrived at the passenger side. He was fully exposed with his private part lying out on the top of his pants. He asked. "Would I like to make some money"? I didn't know. What I had to do to earn the money? But I had an idea. It was something that I wouldn't like. So I became a shadow; some would call; it running scared. Therefore, I never told anyone about the encounter. On the other hand, he cared less about how I felt. So the torture continued.

In-between the terrible pains, my thoughts would drift off to my older sisters. I knew by now… They were looking all over for me. Consequently, I tried to bring my offer back to table. Again he responded, "When I finish with you. I will let you show me. Where they are"? For the second time, I learned that he had the upper hand. This time I understood him clearly. He had no true intentions on setting me free. Subsequently again, I began to scream and hallow. He threatened that if I continued. "He would kill me". Without a doubt, I believed him. By this time, my intellectual level had caught up. I was convinced. This was part of his original plan. Moreover, it was his true agenda. With the ball back in my corner, I utilized this time for prayer and supplication. It had been brought back to my attention. The devil couldn't harm me, if he couldn't hear me praying. So silently, I drifted into the closet of my mind, and called upon God, and the pains lighten up. This was a plus in my favor.

During this time, I asked God for one thing. I requested God to give peace to my mother. It was important that she was able to view my remains. No doubt, she would be broken. On the contrary, I was certain; the unknown would have killed her. I had seen her in action, and knew worrying was her weakness. Afterwards, I let the devil have his way. I began to relax and befriend the devil himself. I asked him. How he felt, and I asked him about his family? He did not disclose personal details. Yet, he communicated brief answers to the questions. I asked. This allowed me time for preparation. It wasn't important to me. What my outcome would be? I entrusted God with my life. Meanwhile, I could tell the hours were growing late, because my body was getting tired…

After I regain consciousness, Oblivious of the hours that had passed, I began slowly to open my eyes. At first, I thought for sure; it was a dream. Because it was no way, I could have survived such a terrible ordeal. So, I remained on the floor in the same place. Where he had left me? Slightly lifting my head up, I began to dwell on my dream job. I would have had as an adult. Then I thought. Models are beautiful individuals without scars and blemishes.

What if he had taken it all away? At that point, my spirit dropped. Once again, I lost the will to live, and relaxed my head back to the floor. Around this time, a voice spoke to me and said **"Get up and get ready"**. Concern about my appearance, I lingered for a while. Then, I had the audacity to tell God. I couldn't leave, because my looks had been jeopardized.

Again the voice commanded me to **"Get Up'**. About that time, grace stepped in and said, **"What about the prayer requested for your mother"**? Immediately, I got up. I walked to the medicine cabinet, which was in the same restroom. He left me in. As I slowly lifted my head up, I viewed the mirror's image of; who I was before? I met this demonic individual. I looked the same. In my opinion, I was picture perfect. Quickly, I was ordered to get dress. It was then; the question came to mind. How on earth would I tell my mother about this horrible man? Upon completely dressing, the answer was clear. She could not see through my clothes. Therefore, I would not have to reveal the secret. I proceeded to check the lock on the bathroom door. Yet again, the voice directed me to **"Move Away"**. Trembling badly, I used one hand to relax the other. Barely touching the knob, I realized; the door was lock. All over again, my spirit was broken. I dropped my head and did a complete turn-about. It only was then, which I saw God in action. For the most part, we have all heard the saying "When man shuts a door God will open a window" I am a living testimony of that open window. I turned around and the window had been propped open.

Moved by the Holy Spirit, I knew. God didn't physically open the window. Nevertheless, I had been granted the knowledge, which allowed me the understanding, to realize. The window was open for a purpose. It was his intention to keep the smell down, of; what he thought was a dead body? But praise be to the highest, God had a different plan. He utilized the devil to make a way for my escape. Consequently, he sacrificed me in the battle, which made him victorious in the war. Once again, God had beaten the devil at his own game. It was then. I comprehended. God had used the devil's plan to put his own strategy into action. Without a care in the world, I marched over to the window. I glanced down below, and realized. I was several flights up.

Indeed, this was a problem. I was afraid of height. After careful evaluation, I straddle across the window, thinking about. How I could get down? Not only was I afraid of height, the window had a water hydrant directly in the midst below. Therefore, the fear of falling on that iron pipe was greater than the fear within. As a result, I relented. Yet another time, I was lead to the window seal. This time, I turned both legs around and a voice said **"Jump"**. I replied out loud in thought. Lord, I know you have promise me wings. But right now, I don't have them. Again, the voice said **"Jump and I will catch you"**. I folded my body into a knot. Before I knew it, I was on the ground between the hydrant and the building. After gathering my thoughts, I stood up and prepared my mind to climb the hill to freedom. There was only one word going through my head. I was so thirsty. **Water** was at the top of my list. Being familiar with the area, I knew. I was only a block from the Greyhound bus station. As I headed inch by inch, the fatigue made it appear like... I was walking backward. In other words, the building seemed to be moving further and further away.

Around that time, a man pulled up on the side of me. He asked me; "Where I was going"? I replied. I was going to get some water. He said, "Little girl let me take you to the hospital". I responded. I don't need to go to the hospital. Once more, he asked, "Little girl let me take you to the hospital". Again, I stated. I didn't need to go to the hospital. After this, he said, "Little girl let me take you to get some water". Immediately, I walked over to his car. I noticed; we had gone beyond the bus station. At which time, I reminded him. I only wanted **water**. Some people would probably think. I made another crazy move. But, I believe. God had set-up this courageous man to be my way of escape. As we arrived at the hospital, we encountered an ambulance driver approaching from one way, as we approached from the opposite direction.

The driver exited the ambulance, the Good Samaritan yelled **"H-E-L-P"**. The ambulance driver ran over looked into my eyes. He ran back over to the ambulance told his partner something. Then, he returned to the car. Racing through the emergency room, his partner move quickly to get help, I can't imagine. What was going through their heads? All I know is that they had a patient in the back of the ambulance, which they were bringing to receive emergency help. Then, there was me sitting in a car, waiting to quench a thirst, hiding. What I thought was a secret from the world? The police arrived on site as the ambulance driver glared into the car. Immediately, I was removed from the car, and was placed in the care of the hospital staff. Then, the questions began. What is your name little girl? Who are your parents? Do you have a telephone numbers? Who did this to you? I answered each question that was asked of me. Convinced, he would return to the crime scene. I told them to go and wait for him. For the next few minutes, there was quietness…

However, there was someone in the room with me the entire time.

Unsure of how much time had elapsed? I could hear recognizable voices of my mother and sisters. Then, my mother entered the room. She could not keep her composure. Her heart had been broken, and then torn into pieces. Through their cries all I could hear was, "I'm sorry". "I'm sorry". I knew they were hurt. Yet, I couldn't understand the apologies. It was not their fault. They had not caused any harm to me.

So I just stared. I was upset that they were hurting. Nonetheless, I didn't understand their guilt. Before I was taken for surgery, I remember the pastor and some of the members of the congregation praying for me. Then, they carried me into the operating room. I am unsure of how much time, or days had passed, from the surgery? Or how long, I had been in the intensive care unit? But I was fully awake, and the alertness was back. In other words, I remembered every detail that had happen from the dream forward.

My mother was there day after day. In addition, our church family would aid her with whatever she needed. Although I knew she wanted to be there for me every waking hour. I constantly thought from time to time that my other six siblings needed her as well. I didn't have the ability to speak any longer. As a result, the nurses kept a pencil and note pad by my bed. Knowing that this was a change in my status, questions started to arise…

I made a request to view a mirror. But it was the lack of responses; I had received that troubled me. Nurses would go away and not return to address my plea. In addition, I had no idea of; what I looked like? Furthermore, I realized. There was a bedside table in my room without a mirror. This implied to me that they were keeping secrets. At this time, they encouraged my mother to try to change my focus. But by now, I was on to them and demanded a mirror. The rage caused my blood pressure to rise, and because of the fear of… What could happen? The doctor consented to allow me a chance to view. What had become of me? It was only at that time. I understood; the war was not over. The battle had just begun.

Flower Girl fund grows; probe apparently stalled

A police investigation of the rape and brutal smashing of a 10-year-old East St. Louis girl appears to be stalled.

But a fund to assist the girl and her family is growing steadily, and one church will have special collection for her Sunday.

Police reported today that the girl is in stable condition at St. Mary's Hospital, East St. Louis, but remains to be in positive care under police protection.

Now known as the East St. Louis Flower Girl because she and her sister sold flower shop and neighborhoods for cars to help support their family, the girl was attacked last Friday by a man who raped her, slashed to her back, stabbed her breast, and gave a wood stake down her throat.

A motorist found her wandering in the downtown area and took her to the hospital. Police have interviewed him and are seeking witnesses. No arrests have been made.

One of about seven policemen investigating the case said that the lack of witnesses is "what's surprising. Somebody must have seen her. This happened in broad daylight between the hours of 4 and 7 p.m."

The girl had been selling the flowers at Collinsville and Missouri Avenue when she left her sister to go about eight blocks to a drug store on Ninth Street. Police said she apparently was abducted and taken to a nearby house on the way.

Police said the girl was well-known to downtown shoppers and merchants because she sold the air fresheners every Friday after school.

The girl has been unable to talk and has communicated with police with written messages. Police said they hope to find out more as her condition improves.

Meanwhile, contributions to the East St. Louis Flower Girl Fund have passed the $3,000 mark, said Sam Steele, of the East St. Louis Chamber of Commerce.

"It's pretty heart-warming considering there hasn't been any attempt to solicit contributions. It's been voluntary."

He said contributions have come in from all over, including Quincy, Chester and Jefferson City, Mo.

Steele said numerous St. Louis area business and financial institutions have contributed. Steele said the family will determine the fund's use. The girl's father is disabled.

Steele said contributions can be made to the fund, East St. Louis Flower Girl Fund, First National Bank of East St. Louis, 317 Missouri Ave., East St. Louis, 62201.

A spokesman for the St. Martin of Tours Church, 9th and Meadowwood Ave, Washington Park, said the church will have a special collection for members the Flower Girl Fund at all masses Sunday.

The collection is being made to help with medical bills, the spokesman said, and in the hope that other churches will seek contributions from their members.

CHAPTER 4

Dying To Live

At that moment, the anger began. I was no longer the eighty pound wise girl with the beautiful smile. My face appeared to share; its space with the bruises from the awful beating, endured by the beast. It was then that I noticed my left eye. It was about the size of a baseball, and had swollen shut. You couldn't imagine… How I felt? I was devastated. With all the strength I could mustard up, I threw the mirror across the room. There was nothing left to talk about. I was damaged and I knew it. The life that I once had was over. Without hope, I had no reason to live. At that moment, I made the decision to give up and die. My life was ruined. My spirit was wrecked, and I had been shackled down by disappointment. I could see the hurt in my mother's face. Nonetheless, she was lost for words. Consequently, she stood there, and I turned my head away to allow her time to re-group.

Although the rape and beaten had taken its toll on me; the hospital staff worked diligently to make me as comfortable as possible. Unfortunately, I had already died. Initially, death had set in; the moment he ordered me to remove my clothes. Then again, I coded a second time when I viewed the mirror. The only hope I had was somewhere buried in the walls within me. This sick animal had changed me into a thoughtless, angry, and a self-pity individual. I had no reason to exist, and no desire to fight back. The one wish… I had was to be left alone. I wanted to remain in the comatose stage, which I had been place in. I wanted the wall to be shut around me, and the window to be sealed. I was no longer the young wise girl, but a misfit adult trapped in a child's body.

At best the nurses used their charm to help me regain self- assurance; yet, the livelihood that I once had was destroyed. I was in a bottomless pit, and hell had consumed me. In addition, I saw no way out. Therefore, I surrendered. I had escaped from the beast; but the will to live, somehow was still trapped in captivity. It was apparent; I had signed over the rights to my mental status to the devil. Meanwhile, the nurses continued to uplift my spirit. They used different gestures of displaying affection. This was an attempt to get me to mimic their behavior. Nonetheless, I had no positive emotions, and nothing left to share. Indeed, I was an empty vessel waiting to be disposed of like garbage. I had been ruined, ripped apart, and recycled for the garbage man. The void that filled my life was cloudy with bitterness. Therefore, it was impossible to relate to other's pain. In other words, I was having a pity party all by my lonesome.

During which time, doctor after doctor would do their follow-up with me. I would only stare. Actually, I cared less whether they came or not. The physical state was all; they were concern about. Consequently, I had left the hospital mentally over thirty days ago. Sad as it may seem, it was only one doctor that even noticed, or maybe even cared. As he walked in to make his rounds, he glimpse at the face of my mother. Then, he examined me. At which time, he stated to my mother, **"I have done all I can do; she is not trying to fight"**. Again, he looked at me; he said, **"Stop doing your mother this way, it is nothing wrong." "You should start fighting and live"**.

In the back of my mind, I knew he was right. So I just looked at him. He walked away. I thought about. What nerves he had? In an attempt to force me to reach out for help, they persuaded my mother to discontinue. Her stay around the clock, and allow me to miss her. It was a difficult road back. But, I was willing to try. I buckled myself up for the fight of my life. It wasn't long after that my health began to improve. I would soon be moved into a private room, and upgraded to a better choice of food.

Before long, the day had arrived. I was strong enough to be placed on the children's ward. It had been over a month or so; since I had seen a child. My face ignited as the policeman walked beside the nurse pushing my wheelchair. We were headed to my new room at the end of the hall. After we arrived, the policeman explains to my mother that I would be safe, because I had a twenty-four hour guard at the door. She thanked him, and he closed the door. I was so happy to have some private time with my mother. This was the first time. I had talked since my many surgeries. I remember asking her for some food. See, I had not had solid food in a long time, and was fed through a feeding tube. She asked the nurse. "Could I have some regular food". The nurse stated, "She would have to be real careful". You see. They were afraid. I would choke. The policeman called out for the food to be delivered. But as I waited, my body was growing tired… This was the first time. I had been out of bed since the many operations.

Frighten that this would cause another problem; my mother assisted me onto the bed. Because of my weak state, my head collapsed upon the pillow. At which time, something rolled from my eye. Instantly, Mama thought the eye doctor had forgotten to remove some tissues. The disruption of what was going on caused the policeman to come running into the room. He yelled out. "Don't touch that it's evidence" he grabbed a piece of clean tissue and securely collected the object. It was later identified as a stick. Minutes later my food arrived, I could savor the taste of the burger loaded with fresh toppings. But

I choked; it was too much to swallow. Within the next couple days, I received a visit from the detective of the police squad. He wanted me to show him the crime scene. I was dumb-founded. All this time had elapsed, and they had not tried to find the crime scene. I was deeply disturbed. With the consent of my mother, they loaded me up to the destination of hell. However, I was okay. I had the protection of the police force surrounding me. We drove the two minute drive around the corner. I pointed out the building. Minutes later, I was back in my room. For the duration of the hospital stay, the days were peaceful. From time to time, I was allowed to mingle with other children, as long as the policemen could stand within arm's reach. At last, I thought for a moment that my life was gaining some normalcy. But soon, I would have to face the outside world. The question remained; how would I handle it?

CHAPTER 5

The Counselor

"Exposed to yet another stranger"

The welcome home was just as pleasant as the lasts days I was there. For this special occasion, our mother prepared T-bone steak, Baked Potatoes, Salad, and a Roll. I was no longer sharing a room with my sisters. Our mother had moved the boys to the back room, and set up their old bedroom for my homecoming. It had been almost two months. Since, I had seen the rest of the family, friends, and church family. Therefore, the private room would provide adequate space for visitors. In addition, it would limit traffic throughout the house. For the meantime, the adjusting period was okay. It was summer; school had recently let out for summer vacation. Before the tragic happened, I was a sixth grader, and preparing to start at the junior high school in the fall. I was a pretty deceit student. As a result, the sixth grade teacher thought; it was in my best interest to send me on to seventh grade. Also, this was a way to prevent interrupting from the other students. Indeed, I was looking forward to the new school and new friends.

Soon the novelty wore off; I would slowly be introduced to a therapist. Initially the first few visits, I was accompanied by my mother. Then after several meeting, she would wait in the waiting room. It would be just the therapist and I. He was a strange man, and to be honest; he looked like. He could use a therapist himself. In addition, his behavior was all together just uncanny. He would drag his sentences, and always appear to be tired. His performance raised the possibility that he was sedated off his own prescription drug. In retrospect, I don't know how comfortable. He was with the setting. However, I knew. I didn't want to be there. I felt like… I didn't have a problem. After all, I wasn't the one that had done the awful things. It was a waste of time and the state's money. In addition, it was nothing; he could do for me that God couldn't do. Therefore, I was unconcern about the visits, and the strange man staring me in the face. The only problem I had was finding a way out of the therapy sessions.

Immediately, I was prescribed daily medication. He didn't even know me. I had no history with him. Before the kidnapping, I wasn't on any medication. But I thought; he was the doctor, and he knew. What was best for me? During the visits, he would start the session with small talk. For example," He would ask me. "What I had eaten for lunch"?

One particular time, he asked me. "What I had for lunch that day"? I thought. I would give him some bizarre things to chart. So I replied. I had eaten a snake. He looked at me with no reply. From that day on, I believe. He knew; I was tired of the session and drained of him. As long as I live, I will never forget the name of that prescription drug. It was **Valium 10mg**. I had started feeling the way. He looked, tired and not mentally there. I had to find a way out of the uncomfortable sessions. I was placed in. For the most part, I believe. I didn't need the therapy. I was fine at that point. Yet some of the older, wise people thought. It was best because I never talk about; what had happened? But I was a kid. I lived the story, if they wanted details. They should have asked. After all, they thought; they were smarter, because they were the adults.

Meanwhile, the session continued. He would ask question about my behavior. At the time, I didn't know. What he was looking for? So I would answer the questions truthfully to the best of my ability. Indeed, the truth was not enough. I often wondered. What he expected the answer to be? Then one day, he explained the typical behavior of a rape victim. This was the first time. I learned. What happened to me had a name? No one had ever explained to me; what the beast had done was rape. It was at that time, my motive of operation changed. I would be ready for the next session. I had all the ammunition I needed, and I was ready to become. What the world had labeled a typical rape victim? Based on what society labeled a typical rape victim, I had to be sensitive. I had to display a lack of trust. I had to dress seductively. At some point in life, I had to become immoral and the list could go on and on. In the meantime, I started to change the way I dressed. The clothes that I normally chose to wear were for conservative people. Also, I had to be careful what type of tops and cut down dresses. I was comfortable in. You see, the beast made this choice for me, when he sliced my neck from ear to ear and placed a stick in it. The transition was not easy. No doubt, the clothes that I was comfortable in would also show the scars of my battle.

I was embarrassed about the way. I looked. Likewise, I was ashamed. I had to hide it. So for a while, I covered my neck up with turtle- neck tops. I hated them, but I didn't have the courage to face the world without them. It was the best. I could do at the time. It would be a while. Before I could transition into someone; the world could accept.

Soon, it was time to return for my therapy session. Only this time, I would change his perception of me. I was convinced that I could pull it off. I planned to allow him to start the sessions as he normally would; only this time, I would feed off his conversation. So I would know how to respond. One way or the other, I was going to be dismissed from the sessions, and I would utilize him to do it.

He was enthused about the session. He noted. I was making great progress. Soon the session ended. Mama would stop at the reception desk and make my next appointment. In- between the appointments, I would gather information to make the next session as trouble-free as the last. Furthermore, I knew that it was much easier to manipulate the counselor, than it was to asked mama to suspend the sessions.

Mama was a smart lady, but she had limited education. It was no way. I could persuade her that I would be okay without the therapy. Besides, I was a youngster with a sixth grade education. There was no way; she would trust my judgment, or risk my life. Until I could find a way to outsmart the counselor, I was trapped. Therefore, I befriend him. I opened up an avenue; he drove directly into my ambush. I explained to him that everything was all right, and if I needed him. I would call him. I had no intentions on ever seeing him again. He was a creepy individual, and I am surprise mama never noticed it. He decided that he would trust my judgment. Finally, he explained to mama that she could stop the sessions, and if she noticed a problem. She could bring me back.

I wasn't about to return, because I would slowly work on, what the world viewed as typical behavior in his opinion of a rape victim. Neither would I allow myself to be caught up in his presence again. Consequently, I worked hard to avoid the things, which could cause red flags. It was tough. I had to be careful about my behavior because; he had turned mama into a bodyguard. The first sign of trouble, I would find myself on the couch again, spitting my guts out. At last, I had outfoxed one of the most popular doctors in my area. True enough, I thought. I would be alright. So, I cared less. What others thought I should be doing? I had learned from experience; what some strangers would do to children? Therefore, I knew to be cautious. I knew how to protect myself. For a second time, life was beginning to be ordinary again. Within the next few weeks, I would start the seventh grade.

CHAPTER 6

The Torture

Hell on Earth

Summer break was over. School had just resumed. Mama accompanied me the first day of school. So she could meet with the principle, and hopefully ease the transitional period. Mama was well- known throughout the community. In addition, she was well- respected. She walked into the office announced herself to the secretary. The secretary was one of our church members. Then, she asked to speak to the principle. There were many parents waiting to see the principle. Therefore, it appeared to be business as usual. In most cases, the first week of school is one of the busiest weeks of the school year. After waiting for a while, the secretary escorted us into the principle office. Mama chose her words carefully; she was cautious not to tread into a discussion that would cause me to ask questions. After the conversation ended, the principle explained to me; "He was there if I needed him". Soon after, I was allowed to go to class.

I was excited to find out. I shared the homeroom class with one of my best friends. On the contrary, I was her best friend. She would do things to jeopardize the relationship. Nevertheless, I was pleased. We had ended up in the same homeroom class. Immediately after class started, the teacher made her introduction, and went over her expectations for the school year. Shortly after, she stepped out into the hallway; the nightmare began immediately. One boy in my classroom started calling me names. They were not just ordinary names. They were names, which would at some point bring attention to the tragedy. He continued his behavior until; he had most of the classroom laughing at me. I was so embarrassed; Moreover, I was so ashamed. I couldn't wait until the one hour class was over.

As soon as the class ended, I dismissed the conduct of the guy in my homeroom class. I had the rest of the day to go, and would not allow one class clown to ruin it. So far, I had met one teacher, which I believed would be okay. Following the schedule, my best friend and I proceeded to the other morning classes. Soon lunch time had arrived; I met up with several of my cousins. More than anything, I was happy to see them. We were all sister's and brother's children, and loved one another. Quickly as it arrived, the lunch period had ended, and it was time to bid our farewells. My best friend and I gathered our belongings, and walked back toward the classrooms. It was time to start the afternoon classes; I remained positive about the students. I would encounter. Likewise, the teachers were not part of my concern. Indeed, the last three classes were peaceful. In addition, the rest of the school day was pleasant. Above all, the teachers were nice and friendly.

On the ride home, I watched as the other student disruptively aggravated the bus driver. Every now and then, I would crack a smile at one of my cousins. Quite a few of them would sit at the back of the bus, entertaining others, at the expense of some of our peers. Despite the comedy hour, the bus ride was soothing. The twenty-minute or so ride was like returning from a short vacation with a group of peers. After we arrived at our destination, I would exit the bus, say my good-byes, and go directly home. Immediately, Mama would greet me; then she would ask me. "How was my day"? I would always give her positive feedback. It was imperative that I worried her as less as possible. Besides, Mama Struggles were hard enough. She stayed in and out of the hospital; furthermore, it was no way. I would have ever added any additional burdens to her load.

The next day, I got up bright and early. After greeting the Lord good morning, I headed into the living room for devotion. We would have a short prayer and song service; before we separated each day. Soon the school buses would arrive; we would go our separate ways. My brother would walk me to the bus stop, and I would head to the junior high school. He was a good brother. But in the back of my mind, I believe; he felt responsible for my safety. Therefore, he stayed close by. Once the bus would arrive at the school, my best friend and I would head for the cafeteria. I loved the smell of the toast, which would light up the cafeteria. We would stand in line with our mouthwatering, only to receive cereal, juice, and milk. To this day, I believe the toast was for the staff. After the disappointment, we would head to our lockers and homeroom class.

Of course, it was a new day, but it was the same old game for the class clown. He would wait on the teacher to step out the classroom, and the name calling would begin. However, the second day was different; he had gained a partner. Together, the two boys would take times amusing the class at my expense. Undeniably, I was flabbergasted. However, the harassment went on the entire seventh-grade year. Over and over again, I was humiliated by the two boys, and my best friend wasn't any better. For the record, I found out through a source that the first boy was her cousin. Guest what? She was the source. Right after, she started bothering me herself. Although she never called me names. I knew; she was just as guilty, because she went alone with them. I was devastated, distraught, and once more. I was alone.

Meanwhile, I continued to stay positive about the situation. True enough, the name calling was damaging.

Yet, the one name would hunt me for the next six -plus years. The name was so hurtful to me. As I type… I hesitate to reveal it to you. Where they came up with the combination of this name? I do not know. The name was **Dead Eye Jones**. I hated the name, and I disliked the boys that placed the label on me.

Just when I thought things would not get any worse, another student, a female from another class started pushing me around. What was it about me that made me a target? I could have at any point retaliated, or caused a great deal of trouble. All I had to do was **speak**, and my family would have taken care of the problem. But violence was not the answer. For that reason, I held my peace. I was driven to disclose my problem to the only true problem solver. I know. Again, I invested a great deal of time in fasting and praying. I remained humble knowing that the situation would be fixed at some point. Yet, the name calling persisted. Not one time was I ever tempted to take matters into my hand. In the first place, it was no longer me that they were bothering. Indeed, they were trying to destroy a king's child.

Day after day, the cruelty continued. The abuse from the bullies were becoming too much. Nonetheless, I carried the burden. I saw no need to bring others into my pain, and share the responsibility of someone getting hurt. I knew from seeing my father in action. What his answer would be? He would direct my brothers to alleviate the problem. But there was no way; I would be the cause of them, being hurt or killed. Consequently, I waited. Yet again my prayer was answered. God had resolved the issue. I will not go into details, but God took care of the problem. It is written **"If I rejoice at the destruction of him who hates me, or lift up myself when evil found**

him. Indeed I have not allowed my mouth to sin"
Job 31: 29, 30. Thank God, I didn't have to lift a hand.
Although mama is gone, she was never exposed to the
burden; neither, were any of my family members. God
had provided the answer. I needed. Therefore, he came in
his time. After all, it was for his glorification. Once again,
I was delivered, and another load was lifted.

The next two junior high school years were pleasant.
I was able to enjoy the school days just like any other
student. At last, the bullies had learned to leave me alone.
Actually, I felt sorrow for the two boys, and the girl was
no longer with us. Her time on earth had been suspended.
At last, I was happy to find some tranquility. It was like
these few children fed off making me re-experience the
rape; one of the worst horrific periods of my life.

Now the picture was clear; I could stand back and
see. What would have made these teenagers take it so far?
It was obvious these boys had low self- esteem, and their
intentions were to keep the focus off themselves. For the
most part, they had outer glitches that would have caused
them to become red flag. In addition, they too were
probably targeted at their previous school, and utilized
my calamity to gain the upper hand. I didn't recognize
them, but they were from the same neighborhood. I lived
in. Therefore, it was possibility with all the publicity that
they knew. Who I was?

I often thought about the sayings some of the old folks
use. For example, "Sticks and stones may break my bones,
but words would never hurt me". I don't know. Where or
how these saying started? But the words were painful. It
wasn't a figment of my imagination. The words were truly
brutal. I have never experienced the blows from sticks
and stone. Nevertheless, I am persuaded that the words

could cause heart trouble. Yet, I would put the teasing behind me.

Only it was not that easy, the boys were no longer bothersome to me. However at the time, I had. What some would call the aftermath of the bully's mentality? No! I was not diagnosed with it; I knew because it was in my head for the next six-plus years. I couldn't face people because they were scrutinizing me. They were trying to locate the flaws, which were left behind from the kidnapping. These troubled boys knew my anguish; they could see it in my eyes. I couldn't be photographed for my ninth grade graduation. I wanted no memories of; who I was forced to become? Two mischievous boys had single-out one damaged organ, and I couldn't see passed it. The evidence was there and everyone knew it. The rape lasted only a few hours, but the agony from it would hunt me for a lifetime. At that moment, I crawled back into my shell. I didn't have the strength to face another disappointment.

Chapter 7

The Investigation

Six years had passed since the kidnapping, rape, and attempted murder had taken place. By this time, I had graduated from high school, and I was age appropriate to stand against the police detectives. I wanted answers; because it was unclear to me. How he was able to get away with such a brutal crime? In my opinion, I had given them more than enough information. To me, it was just not logical. How on earth could he have pulled it off? The kidnapping took place on Friday evening in broad daylight. I knew that people saw him, because the cops verbalized it to my mother. They said, "They heard the screams". But what kind of human being, could have heard the cries from a child, or anyone else and ignored them? Was it possible? They knew more than; they were telling? I wanted answers, and there was only one place. I could get them.

I walked into the police department. I identified myself, and I explained the purpose of my visit. It was at that time; I requested to view the files from the rape. Sad as it sound, I didn't trust them, because quite a few times. I picked out a mug shot. Each time, they would tell me "It couldn't have been him". So one day, I asked them; how do you know? They replied, "He has a beard and you said he was clean cut" but it had been several months, and I know some people grow hair faster than others. Since that day, I had doubt about the investigation.

Another time, I talked to one of the detectives that had worked the case. I explained to him that I was unable to retrieve the records. He stated, "I promise I will get them for you; and I want have any problems". Therefore, I waited, but the wait was in vain. All the promises, they made were untrue. They weren't honest with me or my mother. They just were not trustworthy.

Yet another time, we were at a department store. I will never forget it. My mom and I were in the store. My dad hardly ever ventured into the stores. He would usually sit in the car until; we returned. I wanted to purchase a dress for church. However, the time was short, and we were trying to hurry and return home. During this time, Mama and I had separated to speed up the process. I had found several dresses, which appeal to my likeness; but I couldn't make a decision on which one to choose. As I battled with the decision of what dress to purchase? My mind was disturbed. In other words, it was troubled. Something kept nagging me to look up look up. It was a steady pester. At first, I ignored it, and brushed it off; as if it was nothing. However, the badger continued. At which time, I looked up and between the aisles. I could see the face of the last person. I would have least expected. I could not believe it. I was having a nightmare in the daytime.

I could see it in his eyes. He thought it was me, but he was unsure. However, he knew his signature. He sliced my neck from ear to ear, placing a stick in it. He left scars on my back that required 48 stitches. In addition, he placed some type of strange markings on my back and ears. Then, he pushed a stick behind my eyeball. Indeed, he could not see the other scars. Consequently, he hid between the walkway; he waited for re-assurance. He wanted to see the damage to my left eye.

Once he received his confirmation, he ran one way; likewise, I ran another.

Fearful of the outcome, it was my intention to run to the place. I felt the safest. I was back in the car hiding in the back seat. It was no way. I would let this guy follow us home, and hurt anyone else in the family. Therefore, I was still hiding when mama returned to the car. We pulled off the lot, and drove approximately a mile and a half. About that time, mama looked back at me, and asked. "Why I was so quiet"? It was then; she noticed that I was shaking uncontrollable. She asked me, "What was wrong"? I told her; what had happened? Immediately, we turned around; the fear was indescribable. I knew… We would come face to face with a violent criminal. In addition, I knew his capabilities; and we were no match for the face of evil. We searched all over, but he was gone. I breathe a sigh of relief. It was not that I wanted him to escape. Unmistakably, I was afraid. My parents would be injured or terminated. True enough, I wanted him to be captured. However, I didn't want to jeopardize, the lives of my family to detain him. So after my parents collected their thoughts, we started on the route home.

The next morning, Mama called the detectives again. They explained to her that "I should have run for help instantaneously when I recognized him". For once, I knew; they were right. However, terror had taken over my thought process. It was after this; the invitation had been placed on the table to view more mug shots. I accepted the invitation and viewed some mug shots that evening. From time to time, I had viewed mug shots, but always with the same result. Once or twice, they had offered a line-up. Nonetheless, I refused because; they explained to me that "They were bums; they had picked up, but it was a chance, one of the bums could be him". I knew and had explained to them that he wasn't a bum. His appearance was too well-groomed.

In fact, his hair had been freshly cut, and he reaped of a light scent of cologne. The clothes, which he had on were freshly washed and iron. At the time, I was young and I knew it. Nevertheless, I was aware of the difference between a destitute individual, and a normal everyday guy. In retrospect, I lived in a very poor community, and saw underprivileged individuals all the time. In other words, I wanted to view some of the ordinary or extraordinary men that fit the description. Therefore, I wondered was it too much to ask?

As I waited for my request to be fulfilled, time was steady passing. I had moved on and tried to put the past behind me. In which attempt, I applied at a home health agency. I was hired; I was about nineteen years old. I enjoyed the bright and early rise. Likewise, the bus ride was just as pleasurable. Once more, I was happy. Nevertheless as the saying goes, "Misery loves company". One morning, I had arrived at the bus stop. This was a typical routine for me. I made it to my first destination. After a short delay, I would eventually transfer to another bus, which would take me to my final destination. Upon waiting at the bus stop, I glanced across the wall from. Where I was standing? There he was staring into my face. He was like a dangerous shadow that wouldn't go away. I dreaded… What would have happened this time? Yet, I knew only time would tell.

After collecting my thoughts, I realized quite a few buses stopped at the bus route. It was my intention to allow every bus to pass by. In the meantime, he could catch his bus. Consequently, I lingered; so did he. Then, I thought maybe; he is not waiting for the bus. About that time, I decided to take my bus to work. Meanwhile, the next bus arrived; I boarded the bus, paid my fare, and went to the first seat below the back exit. I looked out the window for him. Yet to my surprise, he was not there. Without much time, I crawled below onto the steps of the exit. I aggressively pulled the bell to exit the bus. I wasn't aware; the bus driver saw me. Therefore, I slightly lifted up my head, and noticed the green bell indicator. The bus driver was waiting on me to push. I crawled off the bus with my knees bent. OH! The anxiety I experienced was beyond belief. In fact, I don't believe any medication prescribed would have been strong enough to counteract the reaction. It was preposterous. The terror was back.

I ran fretfully over to the department store. I erratically dial my home number, **271-1193**. Mama answered the telephone. She knew from the sound of my voice. Something was wrong. I told her. What had happened? She placed me on hold, and she called the police department. By now, three -way calling was popular. So, she placed us all on one common line. Again, I repeated the story, the detectives listened, but it was his response that worried me. He replied, "She doesn't have anything to worry about; he knows; we are looking for him".

At that point, I had enough. I was blown away by the response. I was no longer concern about them helping me. I had to protect my own self. Minutes later, my parents' pick me up, and drop me off at my client's home. For the next few months or so, I received a ride to work. I couldn't imagine. What his plans were for me? Nonetheless, I had my own agenda. I was taking back my life. However, it wouldn't be easy...

CHAPTER 8

Healing

The thought was a great inspiration. Yet I knew. I had a rough road ahead. But, I was clueless on how to fix it. I would find myself stumbling through life making blunders after blunders. I had to find a way to stop allowing the past to dictate my future. I knew that in order to change my life. My way of thinking had to cease. In other words, I would have to iron out the rough patches. As you probably guess, the healing didn't start right away. It was a gradual process. I was a young adult trapped in a twelve year-old body. I was immature, and permitted the preteen trapped within me to make my decisions. Although the thought was there, the actions hadn't caught up. Meanwhile, life was still moving forward. I knew that somehow. I had to find independence.

At this point, I was twenty-one, and the mother of one child. This was the first time. I was sexual touch since the beast. It was the worst experience of my life. In addition, it was a bad choice, because it was outside of the will of God. I vowed from that day forward. I would raise my child healthy, and be a positive role model. Indeed, she was my offspring. In addition, she was a gift from God. For the next two-years and ten months, I enjoyed the time. I was able to spend with her. It was just the two of us. Then one-day, I made another hasty decision. There was this neighbor. He was an attractive young man. We would flirt around with each other. But, I had no intention on being sexually involved with him. On the contrary, he had a diverse plan.

One day, he invited me to come over for a visit. It wasn't unusual for me to go next door. Many times, I would play with his sisters. They were younger than I was, but for some reason, I always attracted younger friends. With that said, I wasn't unaware. His sisters weren't home. He forced himself upon me. It changed my world. I was angry and more than anything. I was hurt. How could people be so evil? I just couldn't understand. Months later, she was born. I tried to encourage him to take responsibility. After all, I had no say so in the matter. Indeed, it was a terrible thing for him to do. Yet, I never disclosed… What happened next door? I considered walking away from the situation, but mama advised me against it. Likewise, I knew. It wasn't the best alternative. Therefore, I did the best. I could with the hand. I had been distributed. Meanwhile, I went on with my life. I had convinced myself. There was something incomplete, within me that caused me to draw close to negative people. I couldn't understand it, because I felt that I was careful. How I lived? I made a choice not to be a half-time mother. In addition, it was imperative to distant myself from the things, which caused mind alterations. For example, drugs, alcohol, and all types of abuse. Indeed, these things were dangerous. In fact, I had witness some of their repercussion.

Around this time, I started thinking about the male species. Not all of them, but the ones I had encountered. Slowly, I developed a wall of protection. In other words, I established a defense mechanism to keep me from trusting them. In the same sense, I began to view men in a whole different magnification. I started developing the idea that all guys had some type of animalism in them waiting to be released. This was the beginning of a new chapter for me. In fact, it no longer bothered me. What other's thought? I had to protect my well-being. I became self-interested, self-centered, and self-seeking. I had built a wall around my heart that was unbreakable. And the rage in me was exploding into barrels of confusion. However,

No matter, how angry I was? I never compromised the love. I had for my children. They were my life. They gave me the strength to keep moving.

They were innocent in all of this. Not one time, did I ever regret that they were a part of my existence? I loved each of them with my whole heart. It was me that I was having difficulties loving. I needed to love me, before others could accept; who I was? More than anything, I had an obligation to the little lost girl. I needed to track down the twelve- year-old girl. It was no secret... She had robbed me of my livelihood. However, the judgment was to release her and let her go. Unquestionably, she had to grow up. No doubt, it would be a mission, because I would have to face myself in the mirror. I would have to observe the last 27 years of my life. I would have to talk to her, and ask her to set me free. At this point of time, the year was 2002, and the violent attack happened in 1976. I was ready. I was a lot wiser, and my maturity level was on target. Moreover, I was confident. I would come face to face with the broken child that was trapped within.

I believe. I had grown up enough, and I was mentally mature to face; who I let her force me to become. But I wondered… How would she respond? Could I persuade her to reveal herself after so many years? Or would the shame cause her to stay in the walls within? How could I gain her trust, and encourage her to go away quietly? The questions dilly-dallied in the back of my mind. Night after night, I thought about. What would be my best defense? After all, we still had to live together. Without a doubt, she was part of my past. However, she was manipulating my presence, and trying to destroy my future. Her era was up, and I wanted her to know it. I wanted her to take her seat and sit down. She would no longer have charge over

my life or my decision. I was the adult in the situation, and I demanded my life back.

It was only after that day, which I was able to go on. I began opening the closet that had been shut for many years. It was my time to live. Furthermore, I no longer had to hide behind the esteem of other. In addition, I found true independence. Most people see independence as being financially able to provide; the simplest things in life. I saw independence as a way of escaping the horror within. Not until that day, could I have ever imagined unfolding the creases in my life. There was no way. I would ever open myself up for questions, or allow myself to be embarrassed by the answers. For the most part, I didn't understand me. How was I going to explain myself to others? These were some of the things, which puzzled me. Yet, I had to come out of my comfort zone.

For the time being, who could I rely on? The ball was in my court. It was apparent that I had to trust someone. Over the years, I had briefly told a person or two the story. These were some of the most difficult times of my life. I knew in the wrong hands; my story could become a senseless nightmare. Therefore, I had to be cautious about… How I unveil the past?

At this point, I had begun to talk slowly about. What the beast had done to me? Not that I was embarrassed, I just never discussed it in details. So little by little, I started telling people the account of my life. It was people. I felt comfortable around. This gave me the strength I desired. Moreover, it was a way to face the horror without the beast having the control. For a long time, he had imprisoned me. He had committed the crime, which I was incarcerated for. However, I received the sentence, and I wanted my freedom back.

So every opportunity I was granted, I shared a little bit more of my life. It was better than any therapy. I could have ever received. It was like a breath of fresh air. All that pain locked up inside of me had caused the goodness in me to elope. I was left alone racing against time to save my inner-self. This person would bury all the negativity in my life. In addition, she would help me face my future. I knew that it was impossible to eliminate the past. Therefore, I was searching for a way to live with it. I started listening to stories of abused women. The strange thing is. I always had an answer for them. Nonetheless, I wouldn't lift a finger to help myself out. Abused women have this quote, which they are labeled by, and it concerns me. They are quick to say. "I love him to death". On the other hand, I wish. I could inspire them to listen to; what I have to say? My philosophy is "Stop loving others to death, and love yourself to life". This was my cue to get busy flattering me.

CHAPTER 9

Forgiveness

The healing process was a start. The burden was slowly, but surely lifting. Once again, I was able to see, the light through the tunnel. I knew. The situation was gradually progressing. However, something was missing. I searched high and low; however, I couldn't find the misplaced piece to the puzzle, which I badly needed. Consequently, I started at the beginning. I knew. Who had the answer? Through prayer, the reply was revealed. Indeed, I had to find a way to forgive him. But how on earth, could I forgive the beast? He was my enemy. All because of him, hell had broken a loose in my life. Still, I was given directions to forgive him. I battled with the most crucial decision of my life. The answer I received knocked the wind out of me. **God**, my father wanted me to forgive the animal, which had destroyed my life. It was unthinkable, unimaginable, unconceivable, but somehow. I had to do it.

I had to find a way to unlock the walls of resentment, repulsion, and revulsion. I had built within the last 27 years of my life. I escaped from the painful torture. I endured by the beast. However, somehow, I had moved him from place to place with me. He was invading space in my home. He was vacationing with my family and me. Moreover, the beast had become part of my thought process. I wanted him out, and I needed him to go away. The more I thought about the tribulations; the beast had put me through. The more I wondered; why I should forgive him? After all, I was wounded, because of his lack of concern for other people. In fact, he disfigured me. I was innocent in all of this. It was his lies that had entrapped me. Nonetheless, I was the one sentenced to a lifetime of torment. His life was probably "Peachy Cream". Yet, I was living a life of pure anguish. I wanted

him to pay for the last twenty-seven years of my life. I wanted him to see the ferocity. He had built up in me. I **wanted him caught, and I wanted him punished**.

For a while I was left alone, God was permitting me time to soften the livid walls. I had built around myself. Meanwhile, I continued to pray, but the answer never changed. I had to find a way to forgive him. Then one day, a voice spoke to me and said, **"Start with you"**. The instructions were clear at that moment. In other words, they were understood. First, I had to forgive me.

Speaking from experience, forgiving self is not an easy thing to do. Believe it or not, I had caused harm to my own body. All that anger was the origin for the misjudgment of other people. Likewise, resentment was the source of me disliking certain people. It caused me to make some of the bad choices; I had made in life. There was no doubt that God was right. However, it was impossible to forgive others, if I couldn't forgive myself. The fact was conclusive. Furthermore, I thought for sure; it would be painless to evaluate myself, versus passing judgment on others. At least, I thought so…

Nevertheless, the mirror was no ordinary mirror. It had been cleansed by the blood of **Jesus**, and reflected a shine, which would expose all of my shame. I could observe myself for. Who I truly was in God's eyesight? I was no better than the kidnapper, rapist, or murder. Surely, my sins were no different than his, and now I knew it. I had been given a chance to make it right. Moreover, I had been granted another opportunity to live.

Meanwhile, I focused on the things, which were causing me to run back and forth, between the past and the present. I knew that it was impracticable to fix my present, without unpacking the suit case from my past.

Consequently, I pulled out hatred. It was packed tightly at the top of my suitcase. My prayer was for God to take it away. Then, I pulled out blame, shame and the list could go on and on. Before long, I was able to face myself in the mirror.

At this time, I could live with; who I was? Besides, I was ready to move forward with; who I would become? The difficult part was over. Now, I had to pour out my heart to the beast. Unable to confront him in person, I had to imagine; he was there. It wasn't complicated envisioning. Who he was? After all, I had a vivid picture of; what he looked like? The last time I saw him. Therefore, I used this depiction as my illustration. The moment appeared real.

Until that night, I had never faced the beast without fear. After all, he showed up countless times in my dreams. Likewise, he invaded my home on many occasions. But this was a whole different ball game. We sat at my kitchen table. He sat at one end; I sat at another. I began to pour all of my sorrow out to him. He stared at me, and through his eyes. There was grief. I knew then; he too, had been wounded. I don't know the details of his injuries. But indeed, he needed help.

At that moment something came to mind, I thought about the kidnapping, and the conversation the beast and I had…had. I could have asked him anything. In any case, he would have answered me. Without a doubt, his agenda was already preset. I was intended to die. I was angry at myself, because I forgot to ask him his name. My eyes ignited like a burning flame. The revelation was correct. It was then, which I realized. I was full of resentment, not only for the beast; but I was disappointed… I had allowed him to outwit me.

Meanwhile, I continued on; he never talked; remember, he was only a figment of my imagination. From that day on, my life has been different. I have been able to accomplish many things. In addition, Fear is no longer a part of my daily life. Also, I have mastered the skills to feel secure. Indeed, I have removed the pillows from the front door, where my head use to rest, and permitted the angels, once again to stand guard. For the most part, I live like ordinary people. At last, the beast has learned to leave me alone.

Moreover, the catastrophe was in the past, which once took control of my life. Irrefutably, the beast was no longer a beast, but a man who made a terrible choice. Even so, he has to live with the dishonor. He has caused. Somehow, he had outsmarted the system. However, his conscience would sentence him to disgrace. In- spite of what, he had done. Vengeance was not mine to claim.

Forgiveness had run its course. At last, I was relieved of the pain from the man that had stolen so many years of my life. It was too late to re-create the past. Nonetheless, I could start over from this point on. I could be respectable, reputable, and honorable. I could polish my present, which would allow me to envision my future. Finally, the mountains were reachable. As a result, my mental status was relaxing back into a calm state of mind. Furthermore, I could capture some of the dreams, which were outside of my reach. For a long time, things were unclear to me. I would appear normal in the everyday settings. But behind the walls of my home, I could be myself, and I was tired of the make-believe.

Forgiveness brought a quote back to mind, which my sister, Donna told me one day. She said, **"Love comes from within"**. You see; it is important to tread carefully.

When you speak to people? Sometime, what you say can be exactly? What a person needs to hear? One way or the other, people's words could be something to motivate you. On the contrary, words could be a driven force to destroy all hope, invading on the will to live. In other words, you can kill a person with your tongue. **Thank God! Her words saved me**.

Forgiveness is not verbal. It is an action word. The action is to forget. True enough, I will never forget the pain, which the man caused. However, I will disregard the blame. Forgiveness means to stop pointing the finger. In addition, forgiveness is a brand new beginning to a new life expectancy. For this reason, it is only when. You have reached this point in your life. You have truly pardoned others that the reward is attained. Undeniably, forgiveness is yours to claim. It was evident that I couldn't change the things, which had happened in my past. Nevertheless after 27 years, forgiveness had turned the hatred into tears. For the first time, after all those years, I was able to cry a sigh of relief. The tears were endurable; because they were sobs of joy. The waterworks flowed down like a lake, opening up the pathway of a positive chapter in my life. Indeed, forgiveness was the answer.

Forgiveness was one of the hardest things. I have ever had to do. On the other hand, it has become the most common thing in my life. Forgiveness replaced the words animosity and antagonism with new vocabulary words. God knew forgiveness would be a stumble block in my life. Consequently, he allowed the devil to set me up; so I could come face to face with the ugliness, which was brewing inside. To this day, forgiveness is still a major part of my life. Indeed, I learned…forgiveness promotes good health. Single-handedly, It was healing for me. Also, forgiveness served as a mediator. In my opinion, people are more mentally relaxed, when; they forgive those that rub them in the wrong way. Furthermore, forgiveness makes the situation neutral. In other word, it removes tension from the party that has been offended, and opens up a pathway to make things right.

At last, forgiveness is like a breath of fresh air; as you ride through the country side. It is comfortable, harmless, and soothing. Without a doubt, forgiveness can turn a murderer into a wholesome law- biding citizen. Likewise, forgiveness could cause the thief to return the goods to the rightful owner. In my case, I pray that forgiveness has change the ways of the perpetrator.

Chapter 10

Acceptance

Finally, the last twenty-seven years were behind me. I could start a new life, and a brand new adventure. It wouldn't be stress-free. Nonetheless, the burden would be lighter. At last, the suitcase was mine for the unpacking. Unquestionably, I could live with the past, go on with the present, and look forward to a rewarding future. Hands down, God had taken; his time to move me to another level in my life. It was time to get busy existing. There was no doubt. I had been freed, and I had to display it in my everyday actions. Forgiveness changed my whole attitude about life. All those years, I was breathing, but I was dead. It was a sickness dwelling in me that even the specialist hadn't detected. In addition, I was the one carrying all the hatred, and holding on to the bag of distress.

Undeniably, I was emotionally ill, and I didn't even know it. At last, it was good news. Finally, my illness had been diagnosed. It was something… Medication couldn't cure. I was unwilling to forgive; therefore, hatred became a germ in my existence. Moreover, it had eaten up my healthy cells. Hatred displayed itself like cancer. Likewise, it puzzled the doctors, but **Doctor Jesus** knew its symptoms. I declare hatred. Can make you do things. You think. You would never do. But OH! **Thank God** for **Jesus**.

Absolutely, the change of forgiveness washed out the old me, and the new me took over. Acceptance starts with being able to acknowledge yourself. At first, I couldn't live with me; because I didn't like me. Yet, forgiveness taught me how to love me. I believe when… You love yourself. You will not harm yourself. True enough, I wasn't drinking, smoking, and putting illegal things in my system. Nonetheless, the poison of hatred was slowly killing me. I had to find an antidote, and I needed it yesterday. The toxic was not fatal. It was just enough to make me sick at the stomach. It reminded me of an ocean sickness. You see; ocean sickness makes. You feel like. You are sick from the head down. Hatred does the same thing. It invades your body. Equally, it consumes you. Hatred is an enemy to the human race. Moreover, hatred can force you to behave outside of your character. In other words, hatred can alter your beliefs. In addition, hatred is a twisted way to demonstrate behavior.

Cleanse of impurity, I could exposed myself to the rest of the world. It was like turning over a new leaf. To this day, acceptance has become a close relative of mine. Forgiveness has made this possible. It has become a popular guest in my home, and a co-worker at my place of employment. Acceptance is an opportunity for me to demonstrate, the details of what true forgiveness means. In addition, I could exhibit it throughout my life. The word acceptance means to acknowledge. However, receipt is no good when it comes to the term forgiveness. To repeat, it is an action word. It has to be expressed. As I stated before, acceptance start with self, then with the people you love. For example, I had to identify with the faults of my spouse, children, and family members. Before, I could share forgiveness in the outside world. In my opinion, the outside world is not always the hardest to live with. I believe that once. You have conquered the inside. You are on to something.

In fact, it would be safe to say acceptance is a permanent fixture to temporary stressors. Acceptance has elevated me to the highest mountain one could ever see. In retrospect, it has brought me up from the lowest points of my life, the valley of death. Acceptance has made my enemies dissolve the extreme dislike; they had for me. Indeed, it is apparent that once I accept myself. The world would be more tolerable of me. Also, acceptance has allowed forgiveness to mold me into a healthier person. It is an outfit. I am not embarrassed to be seen in. Also, it is company, which would be comfortable to keep. Besides, forgiveness could be used for any occasion. At last, forgiveness removed the negativity from my life, which allowed me to move forward. As well, Acceptance is the insurance policy, which will keep me from looking back. Forgiveness and acceptance were the two things, along with the grace of God, which changed my life for the better. All those years, **God** knew the answer. However, he was waiting on me to ask the question. **How remarkable? God is**.

Moreover, Acceptance was not only a breakthrough for me. Without reservation, it was a chance to teach others about the love of Christ. Furthermore, acceptance was a chance to show others true forgiveness in the real sense of the word. Acceptance is a major factor in the healing process. Unaccompanied, it states maturity as an authentic sense of growth. Then, acceptance allowed the ingredient of forgiveness to sweeten my life. For a long time, the bitterness within was provoking me to misbehave in ways; which were unlike **God**. But one day, **God** changed all that anger into a smile. For me, it was the beginning of a brand new world. Indeed, it was a beautiful transition. Consequently, I can tell humanity; Acceptance changed my complete life.

For the most part, it is hard to speak about acceptance without thinking about forgiveness. In my case, they are intertwined. By the same token, they are equal. In essence, acceptance and forgiveness are blood relatives. Forgiveness released me from the burden. In the same manner, acceptance took away the shame. In other words, it is impossible to have the characteristics of one, and not the other, no matter… What the world say? Once again, therapy came in the form of forgiveness. It was the only pill. I needed. Indeed, the emotional stress was over. I could move on with the rest of my life. It was a celebration worth waiting for. Finally, the pity party had turned into a festivity, which I could proudly invite everyone to relish. To this day, the invitation remains and opened door policy. It states. **Welcome to the new me**.

As a result of the forgiveness, I was able to understand life in the dose. It had been given. I realized; life offered no guarantees. In reality, life is like a roller coaster. There are high moments, and then, there are low moments. In the high moments, life works in your favor. On the contrary, the low moment's life weighs. You down. It is during these times, which forgiveness helps to balance the scale. In life, diverse things happen to different individuals. Some things transpire to slow us down. Then, some things materialize to wake us up again. I am so glad. **God** has the last say so, when it comes down to our lives. For a while, things were mystifying for me. Yet, I knew **God** was still there. He was waiting on me to respond to his call. All the time, the ball was in my court, and he was waiting on me to meet him on common ground.

True enough, **God** wants to be head of our lives. But, he refuses to invade our space. Although, the welcome mat is there; he wants us to open the door of our hearts, and allow him to come in. No doubt all those years, **God** was patiently waiting on me to ask for his help. But I was stubborn-hearted. I tried to mend the situation on my own. Consequently, I had caused a disaster out of something, which could have been resolved a long time ago. Meanwhile, **God** understood for **"His ways or not**

our ways". Definitely, I can say a lesson learned. You can't out- think **God**; nor can you take his place in life. He is there for guidance, and when we choose to travel without him. We should expect delays... I am a witness; he is always on time.

You see. **God** didn't only use the devil to gain the victory in the situation. He gave him space in my life, for another 27 years, because of my heart-hard. Then, he put him back in his place. I am proud to serve as a witness to the best prosecutor, the world would ever know. The finest Judge the world would ever face. Above all, the greatest **God** the world would ever behold. In the words of the Prophet Job, "Blessed is the name of the Lord".

CHAPTER 11

Closure

For me 1976, was a challenging year, however, it was gone, and so was the pain. It was time for me to live, and let live. The negative past had been exchanged for a positive future, which I would someday share with the rest of the world. The incident that once caused so much destruction had become a harmless testimony, for the rest of the world to behold. It was a perfect ending for such a horrific crime. For most people, the conclusion is when the perpetrator(s) is sentence to life or death. However, I have learned. Revenge is **God's** work. In fact, there is no punishment on earth that is greater than **God's** fury. Closure had begun the day. I learned. What true forgiveness was really about? The end was a start of a new beginning, and no judgment is worth trading in the peace of mind, which I have now.

Furthermore, closure means diverse things to different individuals. In my opinion, the conclusion started with forgiveness. Forgiveness aided me in accepting; what had occurred? As a result, the end is peace. Therefore, I was lacking emotional peace. The hatred that I had developed for the perpetrator was so overwhelming; it had consumed my tranquility. Meanwhile, it was impossible for me to be content. At the same time, the lack of concern for the next person didn't matter either. In other words, "Misery loves company". Then, closure dressed up the old behavior, and granted me a new appearance in a mental sense. It was unmistakable; change had created the new me. In fact, modification started within. At which point, fear had been replaced by courage. Hated had been restored by love. Indeed, the large stumbling blocks in my life had become miniature stepping stones to overcome.

No doubt, closure unleashed many doorways in my life, which for so long were inaccessible. The hurt had caused the doors to be blocked, by the hatred that had devoured me. Mentally, I was no longer living there; I had been eaten alive, and only my physical state remained. The psychological adjustment was the key factor to a new beginning. And as a result of the change, I regained hope. At last, the mountains were reachable. Once more, forgiveness had revived me. Acceptance granted me peace of mind. Moreover, hope was my life- saver. True enough, forgiveness is a form of fiber, when it is used properly; it keeps your body cleanse from all impurities. No doubt, closure was the end result of many unconstructive things in my life. Equally, it was the beginning of a fresh start. Meanwhile, I can't replace the twenty-seven years of baggage. But I can release it from my care; consequently, it is no longer my burden. I repeat. The end was my start, of a new beginning.

MY PRAYER

Gracious father, how awesome is your name? Lord I come before your throne with thanksgiving. Lord I come with a bowed down head, knowing; you are the only one that can lift it up. I ask Lord that you would forgive me of my many sins, and short -comings.

I ask you Lord to remove every mountain that stands in my way. I ask you Lord to create in me a clean heart, and renew the right spirit in me.

Then, I pray lord that you would work on the heart of my love ones. I submit them into your hands. Lord I know that I can't change them, neither can I change myself. But I believe that you can; for it says in your word, **"Ask and it shall be given, seek and ye shall find, knock and the door shall be open unto you"** Lord I am asking. I am seeking you out, and Lord at the windows of heaven; I am knocking.

Now Lord, I pray for my children and grandchildren. I pray that you shield them from danger. I pray Lord that they too will learn to trust you. I pray Lord that they learn to place their burdens on you. I pray Lord that this story will become an eye-opener, and not a discouragement. I pray Lord that they seek you out, while you can be found.

Next, I pray for the sick and shut-in. I pray that you will heal their bodies in the name of Jesus. Although, I realize that some people are not to be healed on this side. Please Lord grant them peace within. In addition, I pray for the bereaved families that have lost love ones. I pray that they consider the life of Jesus, God's only son.

Today I stand in prayer for the perpetrator. I pray that he has change his ways. I pray Lord that he has found comfort in you. The only heart regulator I know. I pray Lord that he asks for forgiveness of his sins, and he has been washed in the blood. I pray Lord that wherever he is;

he finds peace in you. Lord unlike some of the people in the world believes people can't change. On the contrary, I believe through prayer and supplications. God can change the lowest of us all.

On bending knees Lord, I pray that you go into the prison walls. There is someone calling on you that need a break- through. They have given up on life because of broken trust. They now know Lord that you are the answer they need. In the name of Jesus touch them right now. Meanwhile Lord, there are innocent people snatched away from their family and freedom. Let them know you have not forgotten.

Once again, I pray that you give peace to the innocent. Work on their hearts I pray. Let them know that this maybe the only way, you can save them. We know; you work in mysterious ways. Lord we are calling on your name right now, in the name of Jesus. Lord please levels the mountains in their lives, if it is thy will.

Last but not least, I lift my heart in prayer for the homeless. They sincerely need your help right now Lord. I pray that you open our hearts and homes to serves these individuals that stands in the need of not only spiritually guidance, but physical and mental guidance. Lord bless each church that is open up in your name. May they reach beyond the buildings, and exercise their faith in the fields, in Jesus name Amen.

"A letter to the perpetrator"

In the event this letter finds you well, I pray that you find a church home, and make it right with the savior. I am no longer angry with you. What you did wasn't morally right? But I have forgiven you. I have no intention on trying to make. You pay for a crime, which I am sure for the last 36 years. You have paid for over and over again. For the record, I moved on eleven years ago, and been happy ever since.

Although, this book was not published in your memory, it should serve as a peace offering. I have closed this chapter of my life, which took the rest of my childhood, and quite a bit of my adulthood. Moreover, I advised you to do the same. I am no longer a robot, and you have been restricted from use of the remote. Your control days have been terminated. Consequently the only life, you have authority over is your own. Therefore, you are wise, release your pain takes it to Jesus.

In the meantime, my heart is open. I am willing to meet you on common grounds. I am sure. We both have some unanswered questions. Besides, I still do not know who you are. Yet, I have unveiled myself with this publication. In other word, I have come face to face with the fear that had taunted me for 27 years. But you see. God got me. His invitation remains open for you also. Will you give yourself to him? It is not too late. Moreover, the same bloods that saved me also can be used to save you. In other words, God has room for you too.

Suggested Changes From A Victim!

From a victim's prospective, rape is one of the most atrocious crimes, which a person can endure. To understand my position, let's define the word rape; rape is a forceful act committed by a heartless individual, which thinks very little of his victim(s), and even less of himself. According to some, "Rape is not a sexual crime, but a control issue". On the contrary, I believe the opposite. For example, bank robbers need control over the bank employees to carry out a successful robbery. However, it is not the employees. They are after. The money is their reward. Likewise, rapists need to control the victim(s), but the ultimate prize is to satisfy their sex drive. Accompany me as I share some changes, which are needed from one's victim prospective.

1). First, I believe counseling should be provided for the victim as well as the perpetrator: This would be a healthy tool for healing. For many victims, rape doesn't stop the moment; the rapist is caught and confined. The torture continues to affect their daily lives. It drives the victim to an unexplained fear. It takes over and destroys the richness of all relationships during the victims' lifetime. Sometime, it may take many years to rebuild or restore life to a normal status. For some victim's, life is never ordinary again.

A). Also, Counseling could serve as a way of disclosing hurtful feelings: It is no doubt that the victim(s) need to be heard. Counseling would serve as a pillow for the victim to release their steam, and at the same time, keep it confide in the safety of the counseling sessions.

B). In addition, Counselors could serve as a mediator: In some cases, victims make the choice to meet with the perpetrator(s) in order to expose his evil deeds. For example, some victims want to understand. Why they were chosen, and why the pain? Some would call this closure. Counselors could make this meeting more tolerable by equipping the victim with the necessary protective tools on... What would be the best approach?

2). Now for the perpetrator, Counseling could be an effective ear piece: For example, it is impossible to truly understand, or relate to a person without finding out. Who they really are? Counselors are usually wise individuals that look for disturbed patterns in behavior. Counselors could suggest positive adjustments for the perpetrator. In the same token, counselors could aid the perpetrator in utilizing the best approach in changing his behavior. In addition, he could suggest resources to assist the perpetrator in his endeavors.

A). Secondly, Perpetrators should be evaluated to see if he or she is a sexual abuse victim: As painful as sexual abuse is… sometimes victims become abusers. They rise above the level of the abuse, which they have endured, and become violent offenders themselves. Therefore, Counselors should search for signs of previous abuse, and create an intervention to re-direct the ways of the perpetrator. By all means, Counselors should be cautious of their proximity, because men are generally embarrassed, when it comes to this issue. Meanwhile, it is equally important to assure the perpetrator that the crime committed against he or she was also unfair.

B). Next, Counselors need to be open-minded to suggestions in an attempt to prevent others from being sexual abused by violent offenders: who knows better than the person committing the crime, how to minimize victimization? As part of the healing process, perpetrator's need to be required to expose the details of their crime as a learning experience, and to educate the public at large. These tools of knowledge could save many lives. Moreover, the public needs to be vigilant in their communities, and play an active role in keeping their surroundings safe. This means. We need to get involve when we notice questionable behavior.

C). If convicted protect perpetrator from abuse or further abuse: It is well-known in society that rape is one of the most unforgiving crime imaginable. Rapists are the most vicious people one could ever meet. Therefore, they are convicted over and over again in the communities, prison wards, and throughout the media. As a victim, I agree. These individuals should be monitored. Nonetheless, it is less than human nature to treat them different from any other criminal. After all, I believe that when you dehumanize a person and treat them like animals. Their behavior becomes animalistic. In other words, why cause more torture to an already injured individual?

D). Next, Perpetrators should play an active part in changing their pattern of behavior: In my opinion, sorry is only a word. Without a doubt, words make you feel better, but actions promote healing. Perpetrators should be held accountable for putting time and effort into their transition. In many cases, counselors do all; they are paid to do. Meanwhile, families are stretch beyond their limits in being supportive. Yet, the end result is. **People have to want to change**. Above all, I stress the desire to want to be different has to come from within.

E). By all means, goals need to be met and accomplished doing incarceration: there is no secret that this suggestion is already a part of the protocol for perpetrators. However, I believe the system requires a work-over, or over-haul. Somehow, the system has been broken, which produces unworkable results, and even smarter criminals. The reality is if; we leave the system in its present condition. We will only victimize the wounded over and over again. Furthermore, it will continue to jeopardize our society.

F). Staff should be vigilant of signs of deceptions: incarceration allows criminals in all levels of crime to master unlawful activities smarter. In fact, quite often, criminals use this time to evaluate their mistakes. In other words, they learn new tricks for the same old crime. Perpetrators are no different. The staff should carefully study the behavior of these individuals. At the first sign of manipulation, staff should follow the proper channels to prevent other lives from being compromised, keeping in mind that sexual perpetrators are callous, cold-blooded, and cruel.

G). finally if eligible, prepare for a healthy discharge, and closely monitor perpetrator: upon completion of all assigned goals, and time served. The perpetrator should be discharged and required to follow-up with counseling, as well as the probation officer in a timely manner. Because of all the difficulties to properly treat sexual offenders, they should be required to continue therapy indefinitely. This resource will allow the channels of communication to remain opened and possible help strengthen the safety of the public. For example, it is plausible that through continuous counseling and the probationer's intervention that the perpetrator may be forth- coming about his urges to commit such crimes. Moreover, it would allow ample time to implement the treatment needed to redirect or interrupt the perpetrator's agenda.

In conclusion, Perpetrators are very dangerous individuals that prey on the minds of their victims. They are unpredictable, underestimated, and vindictive predators. Without a doubt, we need to find a way to correct the behavior of the perpetrator. Therefore, there should be no shortage of employees for this assignment. This is America and we pay a substantial amount of money for professional athletics, actors, and actresses. Yet, we spend the bare minimum to protect America's women and children. In fact, we have cameras all over the cities to assist in traffic violations. So the question is: Where are the cameras to help capture the crimes, which are committed on a daily basis? As citizens, we need to make our politicians accountable. But until then, what do we do to soften the cries of the victims? Do we wait while our politicians plunder over the best approach to protect society? Or do we rally for a change, as perpetrators continue to break down the walls of justice, invading our children's playgrounds, and disrupting the lives of many innocent individuals. The question remains. How do we avoid being prisoned in our own society? As citizens, the ball is in our court. **Change starts with us.**

HE Touched Me A Long Time Ago!

I stand before you today to give honor to my best friend. Jesus is a man that will stand by you through thick and thin. I stand before you today, because I have a testimony to give. Not because I am important, but because my savior lives. I have known him for a long time; he is acquainted with me. He's the one that loosen my shackles and set me free. Oh! He's no stranger to me or the people that live in my home. He supports me when I am right, and chastise me when I am wrong. I know. What I am talking about? He's made me very wise. Nothing slips upon me; he sends me visions. So I need not be surprise.

He's been a dear friend of mine since the days of old. Oh! How I love Jesus; he is worth more than gold. My parents introduce me to him when I was a young girl. They told me; "I would need him as I grew older in this old world". I got a chance to see. What his powers would do? I was lying there on my death bed, when Jesus said **"Come on! I have a mission for you"**. Doctors saw no hope; they had done all that medicines could do. But silently mom and dad continued in prayer, yet doctors had no clue. They knew no earthly doctor could raise me from the bed. So, they challenged the Lord's promise; he did exactly. What he said?

Everybody needs their own relationship with God. So they can see; what he can do?

I just need one witness. Want he lift you up, if you ask him to?

I am here to tell you for I want the world to know.

He is a God of miracles; because he touched me a long time ago…

Rape Victims Do Survive!

You have been forced by someone that is really vexed.
You have been overpowered by him to go to bed and have sex.
You have been forced to do something. You didn't want to do.
You have been sexually violated and abused too.

You are left alone; but you don't know what to do.
You reported it to the authorities, but they don't believe you.
Now, it happens so much; you wonder. Is it a game people play?
Or is it the fact that some people like hurting other's this way?

You wonder; why they're not out there with the ladies that are trying to please?
After all, this is their occupation; they aim to satisfy, and not to tease.
Evidently they love it, or they wouldn't be there.
It should be your choice to be intimate, but to be violated it's just not fair.

Somehow, we have to stop them, if we want to stay alive.
Sooner or later, they will be caught; after all, Rape victims do survive.

God Heard My Cry!

I am not a critic, but I would like to say. God help the condition that the world is in today. I look around each day of my life. I think about the pain, agony, and strife. Just think if you were in the position, which I see the world to be. You would be confused just like me.

Just think if you could live in my place for just one day.
You would understand. Why I feel this way?
Yes, I am a writer a very good observer. You see.
I can feel your vibes. You don't care about me.

Sometimes, life deals you a difficult hand.
The people you believe love you… don't understand.
It could really change the perception from the person that you are.
It could take away the trust, which you had developed thus far.

I am speaking from experience. I have been there before.
It is nothing like a sinking ship in the middle of the shore.
Hey, you should smile with me; because I am not down at all.
It took quite some time to heal, but God heard my call.

I Know Who You Are!

You have hurt me and maybe not for the last time. But, God is going to pay you back for your evil crime. You have bruised me from head to toe. I didn't recognize you, but my heavenly father knows. You did so many dreadful things to me. You tried to take away my eyesight. So I could not see. You tortured me. You tried to damage my health. You left me lying there in seclusion; so I could bleed to death.

You placed marks on me that will never go away.
But, I have the faith down the line that you will pay for it someday.
You hurt me badly. I could do nothing but cry.
I submitted to your demands, without even asking. Why?

You held me for several hours against my will.
I tried to offer you my money; but, you refused. You said no deal.
I know by now. You know every move. I make.
You better ask God for forgiveness. Or you will burn in his lake.

I know… You left me there dying, while you were preparing my grave.
I hadn't given up on Jesus. I knew… he could save.
You hurt me very badly. Yet, I am not out to make war.
I know the devil when I see him. The devil is who you are.

The Legacy of the Flower Girl!

1976, was a sad year for me, it brought about a many tears. But today, I stand before you with my head up high. Yet it took many years.

I am no longer strap down by fear. Freedom is my alarm. The terror of the beast is behind me and no longer can do me harm.

The shackles have been released, and I have been given the key.

The fear that once haunted me at last has set me free.

I settled my claim with fear; I returned it's remote to the rack. The final verdict was forgiveness. Now, I've been granted my life back.

The weapon that once held me hostage has been banned from the predators use.

He can't hurt me anymore; I've been released of his abuse. I have lifted my head up high and wiped away all the shame. I have unveiled my face to the world, and I have taken back my name.

True enough 1976 was a dark time, it made me feel blue. Indeed, my heart was broken; it yearned as if I had the flu. But in-spite of what I've been through, I still say God's the best.

He remains a permanent resident in my life, a very special guest. Often times in life things happen to make your existence change. Every now and then the situation is so devastating, that cause society for your safety, to change your name. Don't worry about me, I am still standing; I want be consumed by this world. You keep me lifted up to Jesus. He is my only true hope. **I AM THE LEGACY OF THE FLOWER GIRL...............**

A Letter to My Mother!

All my life you were there day after day.
There are so many things. I wish to express but have very
little time to say.
You have been a true gift to me, and I am very happy to
have you by my side
No matter where in life I'm going; you can tag along for
the ride.

Sometimes it's achieving a goal; other times it's making
a mistake.
Yet regardless of what occurs, you always take time for a break.
Often times I know. I disappoint you and step outside
of myself.
I thank you for your guidance and all of your help.

It may have taken me a bit longer to notice. But now I see.
Your love is true affection and you truly care about me.
So I conclude my note and bring it to an end.
I love you most of all; my mother and my friend.

Best Wishes,
Dionna Brown
02/29/13

Heart to Heart!

There are so many ways to express the way. I truly feel. But they would all mean one thing, love. From the time, I was old enough to remember. You have always been a shoulder to cry on, a listen ear, and a special friend. I love you more than words can ever say. You are a true blessing to me. I am so blessed to have you as a mother. I love you!

Submitted by,
Donna M. Brown
2/29/2013

A Walk Down Memory Lane!

Identity Crisis!

I would like to talk about the color of my skin. The color of my skin tells the world a great deal about me. Some would probably say. I came from a strong generations of hardworking people. Born in the early 1960's, I grew up encountering many prejudice individuals. For quite a few people, it would be easy to define the word bigotry as a dislike toward others of another race because of the texture of their skin. Nevertheless, I witness another form of discrimination, light brown against dark brown. The difference was undeniable...

You see; it never mattered to me that other people thought. I was the darkest child of the seven children my parents conceived. I was confident that my parents loved me as much as my other siblings. Sometimes, I thought even more; but as I approached school age, I began to feel sheltered because of the name calling, and the diversities made regarding the darker children. There was no doubt.. I was dark; but I didn't need a constant reminder of: how dark I was?

Year after year the torture continued. I had the difficult task of finding that one true friend. Somehow, it appeared that even the teachers were favorable of the lighter complexion children. At that time, square dancing was a popular gym sport, and the dark children were the last to be chosen. There was no way to justify. What I felt? I had to face reality, dark skin children were... **Out.**

Being from a family whose frames were relatively small genetically, I stood tall above the majority of the children in my classroom. It didn't bother me that I was taller. Even though at times, it appeared to be a little unusual. So little by little, the children utilized their unconstructive criticism to bring me down to their size. My height was something. I never focused on. However, my classmates exploited it as a way of comparing me to a human skyscraper. In the least, I felt; they had nothing else to talk about. Nonetheless, it was much easier for me to digest the negative comments about my height; than it was to face the dark perception. I had begun to develop within.

As I struggled to find the acceptance everyone wished for, I was faced with yet another issue. I was too thin to fit in. The children employed this as a constant reminder that I was only skin draped over bones. They verbalized such mean words to describe the dimension of my body. For example, I can recall being called name like "skinny, toothpick, pencil, and skeleton" and the list could go on and on. Searching for a brighter day, I dreamed of peaceful moments. It was my way of escaping the torture.

In fact, I was content with the way; my body was proportioned. Up until that point, I had never really taken the time to compare the size of my body, against the measurement of other people. Moreover, I was taught to accept myself. The way the creator had molded me to be. Nevertheless, I began to crawl into a shell as the teasing persisted. Meanwhile, I developed a different perception of; who I was? Also, where in life I belong?

I began to view myself in the mirror of low self-esteem; as I wrestled to regain the identity, which had slowly been stolen away from me. I searched for the inner strength, which had been placed in me to redefine… Who I truly was? Soon, I remembered. It was not the outer appearance that would determine. Who I was? Neither was it the proportion of my body, nor the texture of my skin. Those were just small characteristics that were passed on from my parents.

At last, the picture appeared a bit brighter; my personality would show the world my true color. It was not my dimension, which would tell my story; but my character that would label me for life. There was no secret beauty in my world extended past skin deep. Consequently, I positively searched for a way to change their perception of; who they thought? They could force me to be. Indeed, the task was very hard to accomplish. These were innocent children; who hid behind their hurt, by causing others pain? They were individuals in search of some special attention. In fact, I believe. They were the ones in desperate need of a true makeover.

Finally, I recognized there was no need for change. It was no longer a matter of fitting into their idea of a perfect world. On the other hand, it was an opportunity for me to introduce them into my world. This world was free of judging people; because they were unlike me. In my world, there were no kings or queens. In addition, everyone had some flaws to repair. It was only then; which I began to relax, and accept life in the doses that it was offered.

A Reminder of myself a sponge!

As I searched for something that would describe my inside, or how I viewed myself as a person, I thought about a sponge. Some would probably wonder. What could I have in common with a sponge? So I detailed a few things about myself to clear up the confusion.

It is no doubt in my mind that I absorb a lot of things. You see; life itself is a master of complications. So, I had to build myself up to keep life's problems from breaking me down. Next, sponges are soft plushy pieces of material, which delicately cleans up a spill or excessive mess. From time to time, I find myself skillfully addressing issues, without defacing the texture of the relationship. Then, sponges are flexible; indeed patience has its place. However, it is imperative to bend at the problems of life; boldly face every obstacle, which is placed before me, and take a bow at each accomplishment, noting that every situation has its own solution.

Now, you may wonder how others perceive me. Some would most likely say. I remind them of a dry sponge. This sponge would be closely associated to an unfriendly person. However, I contend. I am only careful as to whom… I associate myself with. While others may imply that I am a weak sponge, because, sometimes, I allow selfish people to squeeze every ounce of patience out of me. Moreover, my daughters would declare to the world that I am a used, hard sponge; because, I constantly confront them to challenge life at its core.

In conclusion, Sponges could tell the world a great deal about me. Some may view these details as positive aspects of my life; while others may conclude that they are only negative impacts. I am sure if you viewed them long enough. You too would most likely find things to compare to my likeness. Nevertheless, sponges are only an illustration of some of the things. I can relate to myself, and how others may perceive me. In reality, sponges do not depict a whole, complete representation of: Who I am as a person?

A Gracious Mother!

It was March 25, 1989, our mother's 48th birthday. Therefore, my sister and I decided to give her a surprise birthday party. Although her birthday was always a special occasion, this birthday was not just an ordinary celebration. Moreover, it was a complete tribute for a lifetime of service. In addition, our mother's birthday gala was a way of saying thank you for everything. She had done and continued to do over the years. Furthermore, the birthday festivity would be the flowers momma often reminded us to permit her to smell. Certainly, her arrangement had been earned.

Our mother, Evelyn was a beautiful rose placed on earth as an angel. Believe it or not, our mother was all the lucky charms. We needed. Our mother was blessed with a good heart to give, and even a better heart to forgive. She implemented this behavior in her daily life. In addition, she was an active member in her ministry for Christ. Around the age of 17, she became acquainted with a man name, Charles whom she later married. Over time, they were blessed with seven children, which they happily nurtured physically, mentally, and spiritually.

Mother Evelyn spent her time providing a healthy environment for her children daily. Outdoor encouragement ranked somewhere at the top of her list. There were many times. We would feel ill. She would remain at the bedside to comfort us. Moreover, she was always willing to give us positive feedback, a way of extending us hope. Week after week, we would be granted a trip to our heavenly father's house for prayer and petition. This was her way of asking God for his guidance. However, there were many times. She would allow our father to drop us off with a responsible adult. These were the times; her health would not permit her to go. Nevertheless, it was the confidence. God had granted her, which she passed on to her children.

Then as the years passed by, her health declined rapidly. At which time, my sister and I agreed; it was important to let her know, not that we loved her; but how much we loved her? We spent time planning for the biggest event of her life. Even though, we didn't know this would be the last birthday. She would spend with her children. The invitations were sent out for the most beautiful queen in the entire palace. In fact, I can still visualize that day. She walked in the house; her eyes glowed like the stars. She stared at the beautiful setting with a smile, which could give brightness to any planet. In other words, she was the happiest, sick person. I have ever seen. Oh! If you could only depict her; as she paraded down the hallway, with the illumination that only the sun could give.

The house was so congested; there were people standing everywhere as she moved slowly around the room. There was our father, her siblings, her beautiful offspring's, and a host of other relatives and friends. Our mother moved slowly through the crowd and closer to her seat. The special assigned seat was fit for a queen. Then, she relaxed at the table, concentrating for a few moments on her surprise. Indeed, the shock had rendered her speechless. During which time, my sister and I began to prepare a plate for our special guest, the lady of the hour. The room was filled with the fragrance of the finest restaurant. You could ever dream of. I declare. In retrospect, the finest chef you could ever imagine couldn't have outdone the smell.

We watched her closely as she patiently waited for her feast. Although for her, this was a rare setting, because momma usually took charge in the kitchen. The table was beautifully decorated, which included a heart designed table cloth that expressed our love. Without a doubt, we were her seven roses, the number that signified her off springs. Also, the room was highlighted by a beautiful banner; the banner stated "A mother is a special gift from God". Then, we placed forty-eight balloons carefully around the room. In addition, the meal was prepared to satisfy all the desired foods. She could enjoy for a day. The menu consisted of turkey and dressing, greens, yams, corn, string beans, potato salad, turkey ham, macaroni salad, baked macaroni and cheese, and variety of desserts. Our mother set there sampling a little from each dish that were placed before her. At last, the meal was over.

We noticed her eyes were glazing at the beautiful balloons, which were complementing her day. At which time, we all prepared for the unwrapping of the gifts. You can't imagine the excitement; she conveyed. As she continued to unravel one gift after another, it is hard to explicate the tears of joy that flowed. Without a doubt, she was thrilled with the gifts. She had received. Moreover, our mother was overwhelmed about; how much she meant to her family and friends? I truly believe her birthday surprise was one of the most significant days of her life. Unquestionably, I know her heart was bubbly. She spent the duration of the day, welcoming, conversing, and engaging in games and other activities. Before long, the time had come to an end. She thanked us… as we loaded up her goodies, and she started her tearful journey home.

In conclusion, I believe the birthday celebration was the most precious time, which our mother ever spent with her children. We were so overwhelmed to see the happiness. We brought to her life. Moreover, I trust. She was thrilled about all the attention. She received. As her children, we tried to make amends for those years of heartache; we replace them with harmony. Those trials and tribulation, we exchanged them for peace. The distress and disobedience we had caused, being humbled was its defeat. It was our way of showing our mother; she had been victorious in nurturing her children. Finally our mother realized; it was not only a birthday celebration. Likewise, it was a lifetime of gratitude for a gracious mother.

Like Mother Like Daughter!

Naturally as children develop, they have the tendency to mimic the adults that structure them throughout their lives. So I vowed. I would never allow this to happen to me. Likewise, I would never pattern myself around such strong-will, old fashions ways. Nonetheless, who would have ever guessed? I would be the perfect example of the statement, "The apple does not fall far from the tree".

She stood about five feet, five inches, a beautiful, brawny woman. In every aspect of the word, she was a commander in her own army. She was the one and only chef in her kitchen. My mother was known for her kindliness and thoughtfulness. In fact, her Character was full of courage, compassion and completeness. In addition, she was justified in every meaning of the words. Moreover, mother was a prayer warrior, which believed that **"Through God all things were possible"**.

Even as a youngster, I would observe the strength that she displayed. In the eyes of the most excellent judges, momma was an attentive mother that valued her family very much. You see, Motivation was one of her strongest quality. Therefore, it was imperative for her to lend a helping hand to those in need. For example, there were times when she would distribute our holiday food among the sick and shut-in. Oh! This was a pleasure for her to share her love with the ailing and distress. Indeed, I believe. Momma was delighted. In other words, this was momma way of aiding the healing process.

Time after time, momma brought peace and contentment to many people. It was no secret. Our home stood in need of many blessings; but mama would sacrifice our last to satisfy others. In fact, I often wondered if; she realized her own actions. Looking back, I am persuaded assisting others was her form of gratification. Furthermore, I am convinced; it was simple her calling. After all, momma's occupation was an angel of mercy sent from heaven to bring a smile to the sorrow.

The more I reflect back on those yester-years, I begin to compare my lifestyle to the lifestyle of my mother. Respectively, I find myself bearing the cross, which she left behind. For once in my life, I truly see myself as a replicate of her mission. Although the chore is enjoyable, the duties will never be completed; undeniably, the mission will never be fulfilled. To repeat, there are many ways; I see myself as a comparison to my mother. For example, I am a nurturer, a devoted parent of two young ladies. I am the shoulder; they can lean on, when the pain is intolerable. Also after, the world has rejected them. Alone, I stand there with open arms to comfort them. I state this as a reminder of; I am the image of my mother.

Likewise, I am a motivator, a job my mother was well-known for executing. I have strapped on the responsibility to educate, encourage, enrich, and enhance someone else's life. I leave all favoritism, foolishness, and fault-finding behind to make a positive impact on some worried soul. Again, I state. I am the representation of my mother.

Without a doubt, I am constantly reminded of a soldier in warfare. Daring enough, I wear the shoes. She once trotted in. It is my intent to keep working to the finish line, while awaiting my glimmering crown. Despite the beliefs of others, I trust payday is coming in a short while. Meanwhile, I will continue to labor to make a difference in- spite of the cost. In addition, I will hold on to the examples; momma placed before me realizing;

"My living will not be in vain". Surely, there will be trials and tribulations; also trouble times, I will have to defeat. Nevertheless, I shall forever stand tall for I know. I will be victorious. After all, God has promised. "He will not leave me or forsake me".

Of course, I am impressed to wear the shoes, which once fit my mother's feet. However, I could never truly measure up to a woman so spiritually connected to such a remarkable God. I speak of a woman. The word fear had no meaning. Likewise, she was a woman that faced problems head on knowing; she would be the conqueror. Often times, I wondered. Why a thoughtful person would have to pass through this vindictive world? Nevertheless, it is not my place to question God.

Even so, I find many people tend to compare me to such an intelligent statue of a human being. Surely, I am persuaded. I have many of her ways, mannerism, and demeanor, because it is only natural for a daughter to behave like their mother. In addition, it is reasonable to accept. Her genes outweighed my father's genes. Whatever the rationale people view me as a replicate of my mother. In retrospect, there is no way. I could accurately be compared to my mother. She was a great person inside and out. Her heart was pure as gold; moreover, you could see the richness in the life. She lived.

As far back as I can remember, momma hands were always generating something. This brings to mind; the special meals momma would prepare to feed the famished. For instance, one particular time, there was a stranger that appeared at our door. He explained; "He was hungry and in need of some nourishments". At the first sight, the stranger seemed to be a peculiar little man. Therefore, my father decided to send him on his way. However, my mother utilized the opportunity to express God's love. Immediately, she encouraged my father to call the man back. He returned and she filled his plate with a hot, fully prepared meal. In addition, she also prepared a dish for his exit. Once more, God had used her hands, as a tool for his purpose. Nonetheless, the presumption that my father had was correct. He had murdered his family and was on the run.

In conclusion, as a child, I could not comprehend the choices my mother made. As well, I couldn't understand the sacrifices. She endured to make her life worth living. However, momma has left a lasting impression on the hearts, and minds of many people. Therefore, it is alright to compare me to my mother, because to some. I may be the closet reflection to her memory. But deep down inside, I know. I could never measure up to such a genuine legacy.

The Aroma of the Memory!

Throughout life, some people are showered with gifts, which they will cherish the rest of their life. But sometimes, the gift received can only be saved in heart and mind. Indeed, my grandmother's biscuits will forever hold a special place in my memory bank. Grandmother, Maggie was a long-term citizen of Jackson, Mississippi. However, it was no surprise to me; Christmas without grandma was like Christmas without a Santa Claus. You see; grandma had a special hand for preparing biscuits. And all year long, I would wish for the biscuits. Our grandmother was famous for baking. I extend an invitation for you to join me, as we take a whiff of an old fashion cook.

Year after year, grandmother would arrive at the greyhound bus station. We would be so excited to greet her. Our parents would retrieve her luggage as we started on the ten minute journey home. Even though, grandma was a treat of her own. I would eagerly look forward to the night quickly passing, knowing; her biscuits would be part of our breakfast selection. As the older folks savor in the moment, I would sit there restless as the grown-ups would pass the night catching up on old folks talk. Their voices traveled from one room to another, while they relished the moment of being in each other's company. This was a cue for the children to retire for the night. I was content, because, I knew. What surprise tomorrow would bring?

As I tossed and turned throughout the restless night, I couldn't keep my mind off the thought of those golden, brown biscuits. The ingredients were sifted flour, baking powder, salt, buttermilk, eggs, and soft unsalted butter. Indeed, the dream was in the making, and I was looking forward to indulging in it. However, the night appeared to grow longer and longer. Therefore, I wanted more than anything for daylight to arrive. Nevertheless, it seems like; sunlight was many moons away.

Then bright and early the next morning, I would awake to the smell of fresh bread as the aroma filled the house like a fragrance. Slowly opening my eyes, I would take pleasure in the thought of those golden, brown biscuits, topped with pure butter coming straight out of the oven. The unique smell would send my taste buds, rushing into first gear to quench my over-active appetite. Quickly acknowledging the creator, I would head directly to the restroom to take care of my personal needs. Keeping in mind, breakfast was ready to be served.

After greeting everyone a good morning, I moved quickly to the vacate spot at the table. Oh! My eyes ignited as they focused on the beautiful set-up, which grandma had prepared. The table was filled with hot cereal, beef bacon, eggs, fresh fruit, juice, and milk. In addition, the highlight of the feast would be grandmother's famous biscuits served with the fig's syrup. Impatiently waiting, I glared at the neatly round-shaped biscuits as my mouth watered for the desire to enjoy one. Upon receiving my plate, I carved the biscuit in halves, covering it with the syrup from the figs. Quickly, the richness dissolved in my mouth, leaving only the memory of the taste behind.

At last, the craving had been fulfilled; once again, I was able to take pleasure in another beautiful holiday season. Without hesitation, it was always a delight to enjoy grandmother's biscuits. However, it was more heartwarming for her to share herself with us. All year long, we would talk to our grandmother, but it was no comparison to the love. She would extend to us face to face. Likewise, the long distance telephone calls assured us. She was worlds away. Nonetheless, we were confident. We would see her soon.

Unquestionably, grandmother's warm spirit would bring solace to our soul. True enough, grandma was known for her generosity and mere kindness. In fact, it was no secret that in every way; she brought happiness to our holiday season. Likewise, grandma biscuits were a way of demonstrating the fullness of her unconditional love. Furthermore, grandmother's visits brought a sense of closeness, which our family looked forward to. In other words, our holidays were peaceful, pleasant, and priceless. It was a time when togetherness played an important part in the structure of family life. In addition, grandmother's visits brought organization, obedience, and order. At last, the biscuits were a way to reminisce about. How much time has changed, and families have drifted apart?

In conclusion, grandma was the Santa Claus; we looked forward to spending time with each year. Also, grandma was our Ho! Ho! Ho! And we enjoyed the laughter behind it. Grandma's sleigh was a greyhound bus, because she was too fearful to fly. In addition, grandma's luggage was the stockings, which concealed our surprises. In the city, grandma utilized our parents for travel. Therefore, they were her reindeers. Nevertheless, she was the best Santa Claus ever. In fact, grandma's costume was a brown apron, which displayed all the love and affection only a true grandma could give. Above all, I am persuaded to believe. Our grandma was truly the Santa Claus… In other words, she was our Santa Claus. On the other hand, grandma was not just our Merry Christmas… she was our Maggie's Christmas, and we loved the package, which she wrapped her love in.

An Optimistic High School Experience!

For many teens, high school is a frustrating experience. It is a time when many teenagers begin to search for an identity for their future. High school is a time when popularity is the one sure way to fit in. Still, high school can be a positive experience depending on your dedication, motivation, and continued focus on your goals to succeed. Furthermore, high school is the first step one makes to build their foundation in the direction of success. Equally, high school is the initial key to a productive future.

First, there are many things parents can do to make teenagers comfortable; as they take their walk through the beginning of their life's journey. It is very important that parents play an active role in their children's education. One way to achieve this goal is to get involved with their teenagers, by promoting positive output about education. For example, parents could teach their teenagers that higher education unlocks the doors for better opportunities. Also, parents could introduce their teenagers to the idea. The better grades earned means trouble-free admission to the more prominent universities.

Even though, there are many other ways to gain their assurance, parents can volunteer in their teenager's school district. They can attend the parent teacher's conferences. Also, they can be a committed member of the parents' teachers' association group. In addition, they can develop a close contact with the educators to be certain; they have the same interest in mind for the teenagers. In fact, it is beneficial to everyone that the goals are set as well as accomplished together.

Next, it is imperative that parents are available to address the concerns, which their teenagers may have about their education. In many cases, I discovered teenagers search for trustworthy adults to confide in when; they have their downfalls. Therefore, high school is the time when teenagers experience countless changes, attempting to fit in areas. Where they don't belong? Also, it is a time. They look for acceptance and reassurance.

Above all others, parents need to be supportive. It is vital for teenagers to have an identity, and permitted the opportunity to voice; their concerns about issues which may be bothersome. This could be the perfect time to address the failing grades. Likewise, it clears the air to converse about all other issue. For examples, the open door policy will allow the teenagers to talk about. Whatsoever has caused the teenagers' difficulty in making the grade? Moreover, this is the perfect time to demonstrate; your support in your teenager's school endeavors.

Confused about decisions, some teenagers have the tendency to make quick and hasty choices. In other words, they leap into situations, which are sometimes above. What they are mentally capable of understanding, without thinking of the repercussions? These are the times when parents need to be considerate. Parents should be eager to hear, willing to understand, and more than ready to redirect teenagers without being judgmental. Also, it is crucial for teenagers to recognize. They are not being singled out. Likewise, they are not the only one, which has underestimated; the consequences of a decision gone wrong.

Just as importantly, parents should display a sense of trust toward the teenagers. Initially, trust should be automatic in any true relationship. Trust is built upon a firm foundation, which include all involved in the commitment of the relationship. Teenagers should be taught. There are things which jeopardize the foundation, and demolish the relationship of trust. In many instances, lying is a prime example. Other instances included, but are not limited to stealing, smoking, drinking, drugs, and so forth. These are some of the prime examples of misguided trust. Nevertheless, teenagers are very alert to the actions of their parents. Consequently, parents should be careful; how they live?

Finally, it is in the interest of the teenagers that parents teach them respect. Respect is like a vitamin, the more you utilize it, the more valuable it becomes. Parents should influence their teenagers to master this aspect throughout the duration of their lifespan. We have all heard the saying. "You have to give respect in order to receive it". On the other hand, the reality is; how is it possible to give something? You do not have possession of?

In closing, parents and teenagers should make a reasonable effort to balance the responsibility. Without a doubt, this would make the journey as painless as possible. Furthermore, it is very important that teenagers choose their friends wisely. Equally, it is vital. Parents learn to respect the choices of the teenagers, only forbidden the relationship on the conditions. It is harmful to the teen. Unquestionably, parents would love to see their children in the best positions life offers. Even so, it is to the advantage of the teenagers. They are permitted a fair chance to prosper independently. Time after time, it has been proven; teenagers have a propensity to follow in the footsteps of their parents. Therefore, I recommend you to make a trail in your life, which will lead to an optimistic outcome. **Good luck on the journey…**

A Valuable Employer

Time and time again, people are confused about how to find their ideal job. Sometimes, the misperception could lead them to the in- between. In other words, many times, they will find themselves in and out of jobs. Nonetheless, the reality is good workers are hard to find. Also, decent jobs are just as difficulty to locate. Therefore, it is very important to value the needs of the employer. For instance, employers need dependable, stable, punctual, honest, caring, wise, and vigilant, employees. Above all, employers need employees with respect. Now, young people let's go in search of how to become a productive team player.

First thing first, employers look for dependable employees. Dependability is a great asset in becoming a good employee. Dependability shows an employer their true self-worth. In other words, dependability allows the employer the sense of assurance. Therefore, employers need dependable workers. In addition, dependability is an investment, which produces a common trust with the employer and its employee. Ultimately, dependability balances the scale within the employees work environment.

Then, stability comes into play. For the most part, stability shows togetherness. For this reason, employers need stable people to keep the company running smoothly. Stability means a sense of levelness. In other words, stability includes the ability to respond to the employer's challenges in a patience, and well-reserved manner. Moreover, stability is a healthy tool for the employer as well as the employee. After all, stability allows every issue to remain on common ground. Generally speaking, stability is the foundation of what any healthy work environment needs. Therefore, stability is like baking powder in bread. It elevates the relationship of the employer and employee to better understand each other. Based on the fact that stability means to be stable, Employees should be cautious not to overload their mental status, and get proper rest knowing that each day comes with its own issues.

Next, punctuality has its place in the workplace. Punctuality is a big word, which carries a large responsibility. In simple, Punctuality means to be on time. Nonetheless in the workplace, the word punctuality is not just that simple. In fact, punctuality is a complex word for any employer. For example, punctuality includes being on time, as well as, completing any and all assignments in a timely manner. Simply said, punctuality is one of the keepers, which guarantees the relationship, between the employer and the employee. As a rule of thumb, punctuality does not end with clocking in and out. In fact, the in-between is also a part of a day's work. In any event, punctuality should be equally important to an employee.

Meanwhile, honesty takes its place in the workplace. Employers love honest employees. **Honesty** is a bold word in the work place. The word honesty is a special treat for the employer. Without a doubt, employers need to trust all of their employees. For this reason, they carefully select their employees by checking with their previous employers, references, and sometimes other co-workers. "Honest is the best policy". However, employers are aware that all employees are not honest. In fact, employers are disappointed when; they realize that an employee has failed to be trustworthy. In addition, honesty is a quality, which makes an employee more valuable. In the same fashion, honesty engages an employer and employee into a union, which only the lack of trust can destroy. As a result, who wouldn't want to hire an honest employee?

Respectively, caring and respect works hand and hand in the workplace. The word care means to show some sense of respect. Respect has a similar definition in the workplace. For the most part, the workplace is home away from home. Therefore, employees should treat their co -workers as family members too; because the co-members work together to build the union to keep, the company growing in a positive manner. Employees should put their best foot forward. So, the company can continue to grow, and the employers could continue to employ other qualified employees. Indeed, caring and respect are double pleasures for the employees and the employers.

Last but not least, wisdom takes its residency in the workplace. Wisdom is a priceless jewel in the workplace. Therefore, employers are always eager to hire intelligent, fast thinking, and clever employees. These individuals are; what makes the companies stand out from other businesses? In any case, wisdom means knowledge. In general, the word knowledge means power. Moreover, employers are thankful to have wise individuals as part of their team. On the other hand, employees are extra grateful to be needed.

Finally, vigilant comes into play in the workplace. Certainly, employers love watchful employees. These individuals are of great significance for the employee. Similarly, they are like an insurance policy for the company. In other words, they try as best as possible to limit liability for the company. For example, watchful employees plays an important role in the safety of company's workers, visitors, and anyone else that have direct contact with the employer. In addition, visual employees assist in observing hazardous material, waste, and protect the company from unnecessary lawsuits. Justifiable, observant is equally important in the workplace.

In conclusion, the workplace is a very diverse environment for the employers, and its employees. However, each employee plays an equivalent role in maintaining the safety of their workplace. For this reason, each employee is valuable in their own way to the employer. Therefore, employers selectively choose their employees carefully; based on the characteristics, they have to bring to the table. Moreover, the employer's guidelines are centered on these objectives. Absolutely, great characteristics are a win-win for employers and its companies. Without a doubt, employers count it joy to invest in wholesome, dependable, stable, punctual, honest, caring, wise, vigilant, and respectable individuals. In addition, employees are pleased also.

A Date From Hell!

It was way back when, and one of the biggest events of a lifetime. Senior prom had finally arrived, and I was looking forward to the best time ever. However, the day would be busy, tiresome, and full. Yet, the time would be spent completing all loose ends. For example, the beautician, nail shop, and cosmetic artist were all included on the list. Besides, it was important to look picture perfect, because the man of the night would arrive in only a few, short hours.

At first glance, the parking lot appeared to be quite bare. Therefore, I rushed to the door to my appointment. But to my surprise, there wasn't an empty seat available. In fact, the crowds extended pass the door. How could this have occurred? What happened to the eight o'clock appointment the beautician assigned especially for me? You couldn't imagine the disappointment. I experienced. Broken would only describe half of; what I was going through? Nonetheless, the beautician directed me to the styling chair about forty-five minutes later. By this time, the anxiety was so high, and I was nervous. I would miss my next engagement. Soon after, the beautician relaxed my hair. The experience was wonderful, and slowly my nerves calm down. About twenty minutes later, the beautician rinsed and applied the highlights. At last, the style was completed and the mirror was displayed. It was breath taken. The color was wrong. The style looked horrible, and I was strapped for time. Indeed, it was the start of a devastating day.

Then, the choice was mine for the pickings. Nail shops were located nearly in every city. Therefore, I drove

119

to the nearest location two blocks away. Unfortunately, it was jam-packed. So, it was important to keep moving on. After all, time was steady ticking. Finally, the destination had been reached. Several people were ahead of me. However, patience would soon pay off. Meanwhile, I had a choice to make. Puzzled by so many colors, what would go best with the outfit of choice? Silver, surely it would take the night by surprise. Finally, patience worked out in my favor, and the hot sit was mine to claim. Immediately, the conversations begin and the longer we talked; the deeper she engaged the file, driving it into my skin. She was new at the shop and her lack of experience showed up in her skills. Oval nails were; what I had requested? Nonetheless, she filed the nails pointed and straight. In addition, the silver was a cheap version of grayish-silver. The nails looked a mess. Again, I questioned myself. How could this have happened? What was going on with the day, which started out so perfect?

Next, the final stop was the cosmetic shop. Eagerly, I raced to the mall. The make-up lady, Creative Hands could bring beauty out of the worst case of ugliness. Of course, ugly wasn't part of my category. Nevertheless, the beautician and nail designer had ingeniously designed me into a misfit. Certainly, Creatively Hands would make it alright. After all, she had made me a cover girl many times over. So, there was no reason to doubt the outcome. Respectively, I headed into the store. But to my surprise, she had called in sick. OH! My heart dropped. Surely, 911 couldn't arrive fast enough. Likewise, make-up couldn't do me any harm. Are could it? Moreover, I was at the empathy of the hired hand for the day. Mercy, I pleaded as the make-up artist begins to work her magic. Colors had to be carefully chosen. After all, the highlights and skin tone had to be taken into consideration. Furthermore, the event was for a very special occasion. Indeed, the make-up artist was crafty. But the colors, she chose would not compliment the skin tone; neither enhances the highlights, nor beautifies the outfits, which I had chosen to wear. Once again, dismay had visited my heart. Sadden could not describe my disposition.

Meanwhile, I headed home. The prom would start in about two hours, and I had to finish getting dress. Rushed for time, it was important to take a quick shower, and start the dressing process. Without a doubt, the day had been very dreary, but I knew the best was yet to come. Baby blue was my favorite color, and I had chosen to wear silver stockings, silver shoes, and silver gloves to compliment the outfit. Soon, I was ready and expected my date any minute. About that time, there was a knock at the door. Who is it? I asked. He replied, "Mark". Opening the door, I couldn't retain myself. He was dressed in a light orange shirt, gold pants, and yellow tennis shoes. My heart bulked. Surely, it was all a joke, and someone had played a terrible game on me. At least, I hoped so.

Distaste filled my mouth with embarrassment. I was humiliated for him, me and ashamed; he was my prom date. Nonetheless, we started on the twenty-minute ride to the evening event. You could hear my heart pounding, as negative thoughts ran through my mind. What would the graduation class think of me and my date? Instantly, my head dropped and tears started to run down my cheeks. Unfortunately, it was too late for a change of plans, because we had reached our destination. Therefore, we entered the prom. Slipping quietly into the crowd, I remained reserved hoping not to draw much attention to the date or myself. In fact, the restroom had become my refuge. At last, the prom was over, and we were headed home. What a relief? The nightmare was over, and I no longer had to endure the shame of a night gone wrong.

In conclusion, the prom from way back when, turned out to be the worst time of my life. In other words, the dream had become an expensive nightmare. In fact, Cinderella couldn't have topped my "Date from Hell". In addition, Cursed would be too kind of a word to describe it. Without a doubt, the "Date from Hell" threw curveballs. I couldn't intercept; fastballs I couldn't catch, and sinkers I couldn't hit. I was devastated, destroyed, and depressed. In retrospect, the day was as blue as the dress. **I was wearing…**

Quotes!

- Just because a person has an interest in heart; doesn't mean they have your best interest in heart.
- Everybody have a story to tell, but every story will not be told.
- The boldest people on earth are the people that trust God.
- For scientist heaven is calculated into their many probabilities, but for believer's it is the only possibility
- Kindness is a dose of medicine almost anyone can swallow.
- Wisdom is the most precious treasure one could ever possess.
- Time is a machine that only the creator can forward and rewind.
- Sometimes life can be like a gourmet meal, and other time it could be like an unpleasant dessert.
- Education is an expensive lesson to learn.
- Funeral directors are much like tax collectors. One taxes you in life; the other one tax you to death.
- The cost of living is high and the price of dying isn't much cheaper.
- You don't have to be a movie star to be famous all you need is fans.
- Even the most intelligent individuals sometimes make thoughtless choices.
- All rich people aren't successful; all successful people aren't rich.
- When it comes to life people have one thing in common, choices; however when it comes to death free will is removed from the equation.

- Only the educated fool thinks; they can outsmart death.
- Wisdom only works when you put it to use.
- Problems are like mold; the longer you ignore it. The more complex it is to resolve.
- Just because you don't want to hear the truth doesn't make the truth less valued.
- Life is like a meal. Sometimes, we get so full; we can't eat it all.
- Embrace your enemies, it will confuse them.
- Any relationship can be destroyed, but all relationships cannot be rekindled.
- Experience is one teacher that will never be laid off.
- Drugs are known to kill. Yet, they have never been tried for their crime.
- The difference between murder and attempted is… attempted murder worked out in the victim's favor.
- Take yourself out of the equation it will balance the problem.
- You know for a fact life is strange when wild animals are allowed to roam free and humans are chained.
- True friendship is like gold; it will withstand the test of time.
- Just because the enemy has the gun doesn't mean; you have to give him the ammunition.
- The oldest trick started in the Garden of Eden.
- When it comes to abuse stop loving others to death and love yourself to life.
- Drugs are an expensive way to abuse yourself.
- True enough, some dealers kill but so do the drugs.

- Just because I don't talk doesn't mean. I don't have nothing to say.
- Just because you whisper doesn't mean. I can't hear you.
- Drugs are not vitamins; drugs are not fruit, if you continue to indulge in them. They will take away all your loot; not only will drugs break you taking away all your wealth. Drugs will destroy you by jeopardizing your health.
- Life starts with conception. Living starts when the bills start to arrive.
- People believe that love doesn't hurt, but it abused Jesus.
- Drugs are just another tool, which the devil uses to screw up things.
- In many ways, employers and employees have the same interest in mind until it comes down to the raises.
- We are all entitled to freedom of speech. As long as, we watch; what we say?
- It is no secret weight is hard to lose; however, sitting on the pounds makes it even harder.
- The heart is a motor only God can over-haul.
- The Government has one thing on their agenda. Work you to death; so you can die before you get paid.
- Some people will settle for anything just to say they have something.
- It is a difference between concern and control.
- "Faith is not just believing your enemy will become your footstool" but someday you will be able to take the walk of fame.

- If aging want kill you medication or medical bills will.
- Everybody's teachable only a fool thinks he cannot learn.

Printed in the United States
By Bookmasters